REDWOODS AND WHALES

Published in Nashville, Tennessee, by Emanate Books, an imprint of Thomas Nelson. Emanate Books and Thomas Nelson are registered trademarks of HarperCollins Christian Publishing, Inc.

Thomas Nelson titles may be purchased in bulk for educational, business, fund-raising, or sales promotional use. For information, please e-mail SpecialMarkets@ThomasNelson.com.

Unless otherwise noted, Scripture quotations are taken from the Holy Bible, New International Version®, NIV®. Copyright © 1973, 1978, 1984, 2011 by Biblica, Inc.® Used by permission of Zondervan. All rights reserved worldwide. www.Zondervan.com. The "NIV" and "New International Version" are trademarks registered in the United States Patent and Trademark Office by Biblica, Inc.®

Scripture quotations marked CEV are from the Contemporary English Version. Copyright © 1991, 1992, 1995 by American Bible Society. Used by permission.

Scripture quotations marked KJV are from the King James Version. Public domain.

Scripture quotations marked NASB are from New American Standard Bible®. Copyright © 1960, 1962, 1963, 1968, 1971, 1972, 1973, 1975, 1977, 1995 by The Lockman Foundation. Used by permission. (www.Lockman.org)

Scripture quotations marked NKJV are from the New King James Version®. © 1982 by Thomas Nelson. Used by permission. All rights reserved.

Scripture marked BBE is from *The Bible in Basic English*, printed in 1965 by Cambridge Press in England and in the public domain.

Any Internet addresses, phone numbers, or company or product information printed in this book are offered as a resource and are not intended in any way to be or to imply an endorsement by Thomas Nelson, nor does Thomas Nelson vouch for the existence, content, or services of these sites, phone numbers, companies, or products beyond the life of this book.

ISBN 978-0-7852-2948-3 (eBook)
ISBN 978-0-7852-2947-6 (TP)

Library of Congress Control Number: 2019931609

Printed in the United States of America

19 20 21 22 23 LSC 10 9 8 7 6 5 4 3 2 1

REDWOODS AND WHALES

BECOMING WHO YOU ACTUALLY ARE

PHIL JOEL

EMANATE
BOOKS

Dedicated to my incredible kids Phynley
and Eden and your amazing generation.

Let your roots run deep, grounded
in the love of God.

You're the now and the future,
and I'm so excited for you all.

I pray that you, being rooted and established in
love, may have power, together with all the Lord's
holy people, to grasp how wide and long and high
and deep is the love of Christ, and to know this
love that surpasses knowledge—that you may be
filled to the measure of all the fullness of God.

—EPHESIANS 3:17–19

CONTENTS

~~~~~~

CONTENTS

CONTENTS

PREFACE

About Me, Phil

Hi, I'm Phil.

A pretty simple guy from a pretty simple country (New Zealand).

A husband and a dad trying to trick my kids into thinking I'm a grown-up.

I have four chickens, three dogs, two fantastic kids, and one ridiculously incredible wife.

I like Marmite and toast that is burned on the edges.

I like to kayak, paint, juice veggies, camp, and write songs. (Not all at once.)

~~~~~

I've been a touring musician most of my life.

I've had the same haircut since I was seventeen (or rather, I haven't *had* a haircut since I was seventeen).

I'm just a guy trying to live a simple life with God at the center.

And that's about it . . . I think that about sums me up.

Okay, so that's that.

Good?

Cool.

So another book in the world, huh? I mean really, there are already so many books and podcasts and blogs and blah blah, right? Why another book? Why now and why from me?

Good questions.

Well, first let me say I never intended to write a book at all. It wasn't some kind of bucket list thing. I simply had an experience in Northern California that I felt prompted to write down and then somehow it kept going and growing from there. It became more like a connect-the-dots picture where one thought lead to another, and then slowly after I'd connected a bunch of dots, it began to shape into something that I could see and that I felt might be helpful for people. I decided that once I'd connected enough dots I'd have it printed and made available at the events I'd be playing at, either with Zealand or Newsboys United. I wanted something that was going to help anyone who might be feeling stranded and a little disoriented in life and inspire people to pursue a life with God in the center.

So It wasn't until I was casually catching up with Brian Smith, Zealand's publicist, that it came up I'd been scribbling away on something called *Redwoods and Whales*. He wanted to know what it was about and who it was for, so I took a shot at giving the clear and concise elevator pitch that would explain everything about it in 17.3 seconds.

What came out was a bumbled jumble of words, hand movements, and pieces of abstract information from nearly every chapter of the book, which I knew even when I was delivering it must have sounded confusing and disconnected. I butchered it. But somehow through all my enthusiasm and incomplete sentences

Brian caught the vision. He understood what I was trying to say or at least heard the heartbeat of *Redwoods and Whales* and got completely lit up over it. He immediately wanted to call his friend Joel Kneedler who runs Emanate Books. He felt this would be a project he might be interested in and wanted to know if it would be okay if he gave Joel a call.

Normally I love that kind of bigger picture thinking and was flattered he thought someone like Joel who is in the "real book world" might be interested, but I stopped him dead in his bright-eyed, enthusiastic tracks. I said, "Brian, I don't mean to shoot you down, but there's no way he's going to be interested in this book because you and I both know that once he finds out that I don't do social media that'll be the end of the discussion. The last thing I want to be is a time waster, so if you do talk to him, just be sure to mention this right up front so he doesn't find out later and get frustrated."

Brian smiled and said, "Sure, just let me talk to him because I've got a good feeling about this." I remember shrugging my shoulders slightly and responding like a twelve-year-old with a good old-fashioned "cool," which when translated into adult means "there's no way there's a publisher out there crazy enough to take a risk on a guy like me with a book like this. But thanks anyway."

So, the fact that you are reading this book right now makes me laugh. God's ideas, plans, and view are always so much bigger and better than my meager mustard seed faith. I'm embarrassed to say that I didn't see God connecting the dots between me, a long-haired, bell-bottom-wearing musician, with a truly visionary publisher like Joel Kneedler who, after reading my first draft of *Redwoods and Whales*, said that he felt it's "right on time for right now."

My prayer is that he's right. I mean sure, I believe him and understand that a lot of amazing people are looking for fresh direction and are wanting to find their true selves and their true places here on earth and begin to take deep breaths and enjoy life. But the reality is that this book isn't going to do that, only God can do that. But God can only do that if we are willing to work with Him and make a move. It's all about cooperation. It's about moving forward, a single step in the right direction, and it's in that forward motion that God swoops in and paves the way for the next step, and the next step, and the next . . .

And that's what this book is, it's a stepping stone for your foot to land on.

James 4:8 says, "Draw near to God and He will draw near to you"(NKJV).

My guess is that you picked this book up out of curiosity and a hope that you'll be moved forward. And let me tell you something: the very fact you picked it up and are reading it right now is a real step forward. It's not a step toward a book or a story or even information, it's a move toward God, and He loves it and will swoop in and take one thousand steps in your direction if you let Him. He's so patient and generous in how He interacts with us.

You may never have been a person of faith and never read a Christian book before. Well, that's okay because this isn't a Christian book. As far as I know books don't have souls, but you do. My hope is that as you read your soul would begin to open up to the God who made you, sees you, understands you, and loves you.

May your roots run deep like a redwood tree's.

~~~~~

And may you move through this life in the flow of God's love and grace as the fearfully and wonderfully made creation that you actually are.

Cheers
pj

INTRODUCTION

Where there is no vision, the people perish.

—PROVERBS 29:18 KJV

Who are we? No, really, I'm serious. I know we all have names and things we do that identify us in some way, but that's not who we *actually* are. For most of us the question of who we are hasn't been made clear. But the truth is, the answer has been there all along and is waiting to be discovered.

If we can take a step back and clear the clutter, maybe we'll discover that we're actually not who we thought we were and that life is a whole lot bigger and greener and more exciting than what we've settled for.

What if the actual you has been suppressed, and the life you're meant to be living has been hijacked? What if you've been looking for something that's been available all along, but in your searching you got off the right path and now feel lost and unsure?

Is there a vision for your life that you feel you're missing out on?

What if that vision is just waiting for you to look up long enough to see it?

We are born to live tall, strong, and beautiful lives full of adventure.

What if we can clear the clutter and see everything—ourselves, God, and the world around us—as it actually is?

We can, and we must, and we will as we open our heads and our hearts to the truth.

This is it, this is life, the one shot we have, so we owe it to ourselves to find out who we are, where we are going, and how we are going to grow as the people God created us to be.

We are born to live tall, strong, and beautiful lives full of adventure.

1

WEIRD THINGS HAPPEN TO WEIRD PEOPLE

If I ever go missing, be sure to check Bodega Bay in Northern California. It's a little harbor town complete with sailboats, seals, and seafood. It's become one of my happy places here in the United States. It reminds me a lot of the area I'm from in New Zealand, and it makes me feel like I'm home. The sound of waves crashing and seagulls squawking, combined with the salty air and the smell of seaweed on the beach, sends my soul to a blissfully happy place. Ahhh, I love it!

Not long ago, our band, Zealand, had a few concerts in Northern California. After the event in San Francisco, we had a couple of days off before our next concert in San Jose, so we decided to explore a little bit. I was pumped because it meant I could get my feet in the West Coast sand and breathe in deeply the air coming in from the Pacific Ocean.

We rented a couple of vans, crossed the Golden Gate Bridge, turned left, and began to weave our way up the famous, scenic Pacific Coast Highway. We arrived in Bodega Bay just after dark and checked in to the first hotel we found. After eating some amazing fish and chips, our guitarist, Ben, and I decided to drive a little farther up the coast and find a place to walk down to the beach. We drove for a few minutes, found a spot, and parked the car.

We headed down a narrow path between the rocks, sand dunes, and clumps of sea grass toward the beach. It was about ten o'clock at night, and there was a thick cloud cover. Other than the phosphorescence of the crashing waves, there wasn't much light. After we got down to the water, we parted ways and headed in different directions up the beach.

I walked for a minute and then sat down on the sand with the waves crashing in front of me. I breathed in the scene. Despite having little light, I tried to study the big black rocks, random sand formations, and driftwood piles that covered the beach.

After a few minutes, I decided to get up and continue my stroll. I noticed I was coming up on a large, round rock in the middle of the beach that jutted out into the waterline. I'd have to figure out how to walk around it. As I approached the obstacle, I could see I was going to have to climb over it to get to the other side.

As I got closer, I stopped dead in my tracks. I wasn't standing in front of a large rock; rather, I was staring at a whale—a beached, lifeless whale!

Not normal.

As a kid growing up in New Zealand, I'd roam the beach and find all kinds of cool stuff like dead stingrays discarded by fishermen or seahorses caught in rock pools at low tide, but this whale experience was different.

This was a young gray whale about thirty feet long. These whales are meant to grow up to fifty feet long—larger than a tour bus. They migrate down the Pacific coast from Alaska to Mexico.

At times during the migration, the young whales can get distracted and separated from their families. Something will catch their attention and they'll chase after it, get separated from the pod, and lose their way. Once this happens they are susceptible to being chased and attacked by killer whales or struck by ships. Or they may simply get lost and head toward the beach, not understanding the dangers of shallow water, and find themselves stranded on the beach or on a sandbar.

I found myself wondering what had captured the attention of this young whale, luring it away from the safety of its pod.

I sat down beside it—just me and the whale.

When I was a kid I'd seen news reports of beached whales on TV but never witnessed one firsthand. It was one of the strangest feelings I've ever had. Here I was sitting next to this majestic beast.

Whales are meant to rule the ocean, but this one

got distracted, wandered off, and got lost, ending up stranded in the shallows of the beach, gasping for air— and now it was dead.

Not cool.

2

WHALES AREN'T MEANT TO DIE ALONE ON BEACHES

I went back to the hotel and tried to get some sleep, but it was no use. The little sleep I did manage to get was interrupted by weird dreams, and I woke up early the next morning feeling restless and unsettled. I just couldn't get the image of the whale out of my mind.

The guys decided to head back to San Francisco to invade its thrift shops and record stores in search of T-shirts and rare vinyl, but I needed to get back to the whale. I wanted to be sure I'd seen what I thought I'd seen.

Sure enough, it was there, only now there were a bunch of people surrounding it and taking selfies with it. It felt wrong and uncool, so I got back in the van and began to drive farther up the coast.

After a few hours of winding along the coastal cliff tops, I reached the Navarro River. At that point I turned east to follow the river inland and catch the main highway back down toward San Francisco. Almost instantly I was swallowed up by the shade of some of the most incredible trees on earth: redwoods. Beautiful, enormous, strong redwoods growing beside the river with their roots intertwined. A city of trees, hundreds of years old, standing tall, drinking deep, and growing strong together.

At this point I need you to know that although I may look like a 1970s flower child—and I guess in a few ways I am a bit of a hippie—it's not really normal for me to get all emotional about trees and dead animals.

I knew something bigger was going on here. I felt like God wanted to communicate something from His heart to my heart. He wanted me to deeply feel the contrast between the beauty of the redwood trees by the river and the ugly scene I'd been shown the night before on the beach.

That young whale was born to roam and rule the ocean alongside its family and friends, born to grow up to fifty feet long, weigh forty tons, and live for seventy years. Instead it got off course, became stranded, and died slowly—way before its time.

The scene on the beach made me mad because whales aren't meant to die alone on beaches, and it wasn't necessary. And that's why I felt the need to write this stuff down. Because, sadly, the whale's situation parallels a lot of people's lives today.

Too many of us are finding ourselves stuck. Stuck in cycles of fear, addiction, comparison, and self-loathing, which leads to shallow breathing, shame, and shadows.

We're here to live for a purpose beyond indulging our earthling appetites and chasing pleasure, and we are definitely not meant to suffocate and take in short gasps of air, feeling hopeless. Here's what I know: we are here on planet earth for a lot more than that. A lot more than for just ourselves and the ideas the world throws at us and tells us are all normal.

We are meant to be in the flow of who God made us to be, and we're meant to enjoy Him and the plans and purposes He has for each of us. We're designed for vision and dreaming and for things larger than ourselves.

The whale scene reminded me of this quote, which has been attributed to several famous persons:

"Many people die at twenty-five and aren't buried until they're seventy-five."

Several years ago, someone invited me to a 6:00 a.m. men's gathering, and I decided to go, which for me was really weird because I didn't like getting up early. Anyway, that morning I heard that quote, and it shot me like an arrow through the chest.

At the time, I was in a band that traveled the world and sold millions of records. I was married to a beautiful woman (I still am) who was on TV, and I had a cute nine-month-old baby girl. I lived in a great house and drove a nice car. I was living the American Dream—a nobody kid from the other side of the world who traveled to the land of opportunity and made it. Success, at least in the eyes of the world. Hooray!

So why did that quote hit me so hard? It hit me because even though I had everything, I realized I had nothing if my soul wasn't alive and thriving.

Somehow I knew things weren't right.

There I was, moving right along on my career path—a path that seemed wide and clear as far as I could see, but I wasn't really going anywhere. I was like a young whale dangerously drifting along without any real direction.

Here's the thing: my life wasn't miserable, I was actually happy. I had everything I was supposed to have to be successful in the eyes of the world, but I had a sense that I was being drawn to a new beginning, a restart or a rebirth, and I could choose to ignore it or pay attention.

Something was stirring in my heart. I was aware of it but not sure where it would lead. But I went with it, and I'm glad I did because it started a redirection in my life.

~~~~~

I realized I had nothing if my soul wasn't alive and thriving.

That quote was saying that people can lose their vision and their reason for living at twenty-five but trudge on without vision until they die later in life, usually in their seventies. I was twenty-eight when I heard it, and it challenged me to examine my life in a big way.

The crazy thing is that these days I feel like we could change the age from twenty-five to fifteen, because way too many teenagers are feeling dead inside in so many areas. I hate that!

Too many people are drifting along with a numb feeling inside that makes them want to hurt themselves in order to feel something. Maybe they even think it would be better to put an end to their lives.

This is an enormously distorted way of thinking. Lies like these jack up our heads and clog the arteries of our hearts, causing us to die inside.

Let's get honest with ourselves, get some truth flowing through our veins and into our heads, and see where it leads us.

It's time to get courageous.

It's time to breathe deep again and take life back.

Yes? Yes!

It's time to
get courageous.
It's time to breathe
deep again and
take life back.

3

I KNOW WHAT YOU WANT BECAUSE I WANT THE SAME THINGS

You want to *really live*, and you know deep down that you were born for a significant, adventurous, and useful existence.

There is life inside of you that's waiting to be lived out! Somehow you know it—somehow you've always felt there's more, and *you want it*!

~~~~

YOU WERE BORN TO BE ALIVE . . . REALLY
ALIVE!!

THIS IS WHAT YOU WANT . . . I KNOW THIS
ABOUT YOU BECAUSE I WANT THE SAME
THING! I WANT TO LIVE, REALLY LIVE!

I DON'T JUST WANT TO SURVIVE . . . I WANT
TO THRIVE!

AND *YOU DO TOO*!

WE WANT TO HAVE BRIGHT EYES. WE WANT
TO BREATHE DEEP.

WE WANT TO BE HAND SHAKERS, NOT FIST
WAVERS.

WE WANT TO BE GIVERS, NOT TAKERS.

WE WANT TO BE LOVERS, NOT LUSTERS.

WE WANT TO BE LISTENERS, NOT OPINION
SPOUTERS.

WE WANT TO BE DOERS, NOT JUST DAY
DREAMERS.

WE WANT TO SEE PEOPLE, NOT JUST LOOK
AT OTHERS.

WE WANT TO BE JOY GIVERS, NOT PLEASURE
TAKERS.

WE WANT TO STAND UP IN THE
    HURRICANE, NOT BE BLOWN OVER IN
    THE BREEZE.
WE WANT TO BE LOVED TRUTHFULLY, WE
    WANT TO LOVE TRUTHFULLY.
WE WANT THIS STUFF, RIGHT?

The answer is yes. We all do!

Like one of those beautiful redwoods, fearfully and wonderfully alive, we were born to have our roots run deep and to grow taller and stronger and more useful.

We're also like those gray whales, born to enjoy the flow and adventure of true life!

We were born to be *fully functioning, deep breathing, adventurous, purpose-filled* human beings in the flow of life—that's who we are.

The actual me and the **ACTUAL YOU**!

» Questions:

Are you being and becoming you?

Are you feeling alive?

Are you feeling clearheaded?

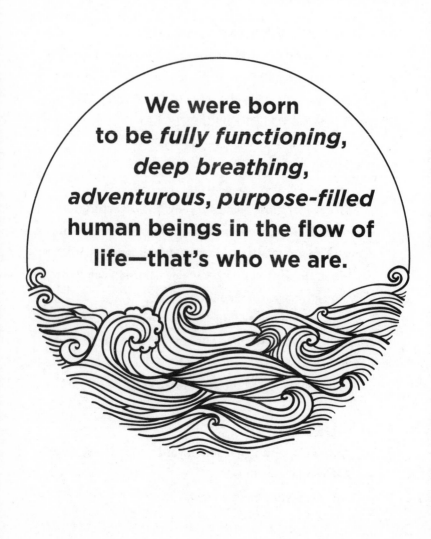

We were born
to be *fully functioning*,
deep breathing,
adventurous, purpose-filled
human beings in the flow of
life—that's who we are.

Or are you relating a little more to the whale at the moment? Tired, dazed, and confused, unable to take in a deep breath and catch up with yourself and your surroundings?

If that's so, I don't want you to panic and I hope I don't sound like a salesman because this isn't some kind of sales pitch. I just want you to hear the truth, because you were born to be amazing and live a wildly adventurous life. You owe it to yourself to go for it and get some fresh vision and direction for your life.

Right?

Right.

So the big question is, *What's next?*

4

HERE'S WHAT'S NEXT: WE GO GREEN

Disclaimer: Okay. I completely understand that there are all kinds of people in this world, with all kinds of backgrounds, experiences, and life journeys. Some are not familiar with the Bible, and if this is you, I want to be sensitive to you. But I need you to hear my heart, keep an open mind, and trust me when I ask you to read on and go with it because this stuff is really, really good. It's about you and God, your life and your mental and spiritual health, and there will be more of it throughout this book. So if you are not a "church person," I don't want you to be shut down but rather to stay open, because I want to share a really cool verse with you:

> Blessed is the one who trusts in the LORD,
>   whose confidence is in him.
> They will be like a tree planted by the water
>   that sends out its roots by the stream.
> It does not fear when heat comes;
>   its leaves are always green.
> It has no worries in a year of drought
>   and never fails to bear fruit. (Jeremiah
>   17:7–8)

I love these words. When I first read them a bunch of years ago, I wanted to tear the page out and eat it so I could get this truth into my veins! It's a picture of how our lives are meant to roll.

We were born to live life with fresh hope, getting greener as we go. We are here on this planet for reasons we don't even know about yet, to be fruitful in ways we don't yet understand. It's kinda like a jigsaw puzzle where we're all meant to fit into the picture and live the lives and do the things we are each uniquely created for.

But if you're wasting your time, then you're wasting your life. And if you're wasting your life, then you're not bringing who you truly are to the party, and we're all missing out.

What a waste!

If you know me, you know that I hate waste. It was instilled in me by my wonderfully frugal parents, who knew how to stretch dollars and recycle or repurpose almost anything. They're still like this and always will be. Waste to them just seems wrong, and I agree. Waste *is* wrong, and that's especially true when it comes to wasting people's lives.

This is life—your life—and it's not meant to be wasted. You have things to do, things that only you can do, but they're not gonna get done if you're slowly dying and breathing shallow.

Some of you are artists and creatives who need to be in the flow of true life in order to create life-giving art.

We are here
on this planet for
reasons we don't even
know about yet.

Some of you are born to be revolutionaries, movie-makers, or businesspeople who will bring change to different people groups or cultures.

Some of you are born to invent and dream up solutions for environmental issues or solve practical problems that will help others overcome challenges in their lives.

And this life—your life—is designed to be lived trusting God. Just like those redwoods I saw in California, you were born to drink deep from the flow of God's goodness and grow strong and tall with your leaves becoming greener as you become more fruitful and useful.

If you're not getting greener, then you're getting *ripped off*, and that stinks.

So at this point I can hear some of you saying, "Okay, sure, I get it. I see where you're going with this. You want me to trust God, but for what?"

Aha, thank you for your somewhat cynical question. And I shall respond with some out-of-context Shakespeare in the next chapter.

If you're wasting your life, then you're not bringing who you truly are to the party, and we're all missing out.

5

TO BE OR NOT TO BE . . . THAT IS THE QUESTION

to be SEEN
to be UNDERSTOOD
to be LOVED

This is what we all want!
    This is what we all need!

~~~~~

It's inside each of us to want these things, and it's *okay* because that's how God made us.

We want

to be **SEEN** / recognized
to be **UNDERSTOOD** / approved of
to be **LOVED** / deeply valued

What you just read is kinda MASSIVE.

If you missed it, you should read it again and seriously think about it.

We want

to be **SEEN** / recognized
to be **UNDERSTOOD** / approved of
to be **LOVED** / deeply valued

These three needs are totally legitimate and are meant to be met, just not in the ways most of us try to meet them.

Our culture tells us that if we want to be significant in this life, we need to be either famous, beautiful, or rich, or preferably all three. It claims that these things will get us seen, understood, and loved, and then we'll be satisfied . . .

Hmmm?

Nope.

> ## "I think everybody should get rich and famous and do everything they ever dreamed of so they can see that it's not the answer."
>
> —JIM CARREY

The thing is that it never works out to where any amount of fame, recognition, accolades, success, money, social-media attention, or possessions will ever be enough. If these things come along in the course of our lives, then that's cool. But they can't be what we chase, because we'll never get what we think they'll give us.

That beautiful whale got distracted and was chasing the wrong stuff, and he probably didn't even know what was happening before he became stranded and alone.

Sometimes we just chase the wrong things, too, and it doesn't get us where we want to be.

There will be a constant craving in our hearts until we figure out that the only way to become whole and complete human beings is to trust and embrace the God who designed us and created us. He designed us to receive all the things we're talking about—*from Him*. He can fill those needs if we let Him, and if we trust Him to meet them.

I can hear some of you saying, "Why trust God if I think He's a jerk?"

That is such a good question, I think we need to start the next chapter with it.

He designed us to receive all the things we're talking about—*from Him*.

6

WHY TRUST GOD IF I THINK HE'S A JERK?

Every big question deserves a funny little story.

When my wife, Heather, was a kid, she saw her dentist, Dr. Stevens, every six months for a cleaning and checkup. She really liked him. He was always nice to her and would let her visit the treasure box after each cleaning so she could pick out some candy (job security for him). He was a kind man, a great guy, and she always looked forward to her visits.

When she was nine years old, one Monday morning

at a six-month checkup, he told her it was time to get braces to correct her severe overbite, the result of years of thumb sucking. The catch was, he was going to have to extract four of her baby teeth so the orthodontist would have the room he needed to straighten the rest of her teeth. The orthodontist appointment was set for that Thursday, and she was scheduled to come back the next day to Dr. Stevens to have her teeth pulled.

She left feeling great about her visit and excited about getting her new braces, which had been a dream of hers. She'd even created her own "braces" from paper clips and rubber bands. The moment she'd been waiting for had finally come!

That night her parents headed out for a dinner party and left her brother, who was five years older, in charge. With the earnestness of a nine-year-old, she told him all about her trip to the dentist that day and how the very next day she was going back to get four of her teeth pulled so she could get her braces put on. Armed with this interesting information, her brother seized the opportunity to do what older brothers do—try to freak out their younger siblings.

He began to explain the tooth-pulling process in detail. First, she would need to be strapped to the chair so she couldn't move or escape. The doctor would then use an enormous needle as thick as a pencil to deliver the shots to each of her teeth that were to be pulled. A large pair of pliers would then be used to rip out each tooth. There would be blood—*a lot of blood!* And there would be pain—*a lot of pain!*

As she listened to what would be her fate, she began to freak out at the thought of Dr. Stevens jamming an enormous sharp needle into her mouth, then ripping out her teeth one by one with a pair of rusty old pliers. So Heather decided to take matters into her own hands—literally.

She went to her parents' room, where the stationary exercise bike was kept. She found some dental floss and tied the end to one of the pedals. She then tied the other end of the floss to one of her teeth and began to pedal. After about an hour of blood, sweat, and tears, she'd pedaled out all four teeth. There was blood and there was a lot of pain because none of the teeth were loose to begin with, but the job was done.

~~~~~

Her parents came home to a hysterical son and a bloody, toothless daughter, and they thought something terrible had happened. The truth had been twisted and exaggerated, and it caused Heather to act like a crazy person.

Okay. Gross, bloody story over. Let me take a shot at connecting the illustration to our discussion.

Heather had known Dr. Stevens her whole life. She knew him as a really nice man who wanted the best for her. Then her brother—who, by the way, is actually one of the coolest people on the planet—jokingly took the truth, twisted it, and she listened. Dr. Stevens then seemed like a violent psycho who was out to get blood. Her *belief* about who he was changed, and it made her change her behavior and do crazy stuff.

So could it be that something like that happened to your thinking about God?

Maybe somewhere along the line you saw, heard, or thought something that was a lie about God. And maybe you believed it, and maybe now you behave in certain ways that you know aren't healthy for you.

Maybe you chase certain things because you don't

have the truth locked in about how God sees you, understands you, and loves you. So you chase other things to fill the needs you have in your heart. It makes sense, right?

Sadly, there are way too many people claiming to be God's representatives who are, quite frankly, representing a prideful, grumpy, fist-shaking, angry God. That's who they've become themselves, and they think God must be like them. They want to feel like they're on the winning team; they want *teamship* instead of *relationship*.

Side note thought: I'm a songwriter and worship leader, and sometimes I get the feeling that people think God wants us to keep singing about how great and loving He is because for some reason He craves it and He needs to be constantly sung about and reminded of who He is.

Really? *No.*

God knows who He is. It's *us* who need to be reminded. And that's why it's good for us to sing and repeat the truth written in songs about Him, because we forget just how good He is and we need to be reminded. He's totally clear about who He is!

~~~~~

Maybe you chase certain things because you don't have the truth locked in about how God sees you, understands you, and loves you.

Yes, He's the most magnificent and powerful being there is, yet at the same time He's the most humble being ever, and He doesn't need His ego stroked. He's God. He doesn't have an inferiority complex. He knows who He is. He's amazing!

What I'm trying to point out is that *if we believe the wrong stuff, we'll behave in wrong ways*, and that won't change until we start to believe and think the right stuff. It all starts with what we think and believe about who God is.

> ## "As he thinks, so he is; as he continues to think, so he remains."
> —JAMES ALLEN, *AS A MAN THINKETH*, 1903

Could it be that your thinking needs to change?

Maybe some angry religious fruitcakes have told you who God is, and they have pretty much made Him out to be an unpredictable psycho?

Well, that stinks, and I'm sorry if that's been your experience.

They were wrong.

God is good and He's for you—it's that simple.

He's not who you think He is. He's not mad at you and upset with you. And He's not standing with His arms folded waiting for you to grovel on the floor and beg Him not to hurt you. *No, no, no!*

He forgives anything bad you've ever done or said or thought, and He wants you to accept His forgiveness and stop living in the shadows of shame and regret.

The truth is that God is Love, and He loves you because you're worth loving and wants you to quit hurting yourself. He wants us all to live in a real relationship with Him, because He knows that life with Him at the center is the only way our lives will make sense.

It's time to lock in the truth of what God says about Himself, about you, and about your life. He loves you, forgives you, and reaches for you. Don't be afraid to reach back.

Okay, before we move on, let's do a wee summary.

Point 1: Some clumsy guy (me) nearly tripped over a dead whale that had drifted off course and gotten stuck.

Parallel = People can chase the wrong stuff and get

lost while looking to be seen, understood, and loved without even knowing it's happening.

Point 2: The same guy (still me) got awestruck by some gigantomungus, beautiful trees.

Parallel = We are meant to grow greener and stronger like redwoods that drink from the river as we trust that God sees, understands, and loves us.

Point 3: Heather believed lies about her dentist, and it changed what she believed about him, which led to her acting crazy.

Parallel = If we have the wrong idea about what God's really like, we won't trust Him. And if we don't trust Him for what we need, we'll keep chasing the wrong stuff and keep doing stupid things looking for it, and we won't get in the flow and we won't get greener.

Comprende?

7

THE BIGGEST QUESTION EVER

Okay, the sadistic story about the dentist and the illustration made about how we view God brings us to pretty much the biggest question ever: *What's God like—really?*

Luckily I don't have to answer this, because Jesus already did. Jesus came to earth to show us who God really is. He also came to teach us how to live and to set us free from the lies that have kept us living scrappy earthling lives instead of being true humans who embrace their Creator and His ways of doing this thing called life.

When people got around Jesus, they were drawn out of their shells and no longer felt ashamed or hidden or unseen or misunderstood or frightened or unloved or devalued. They experienced the opposite. Suddenly they knew they were *seen* and *understood* and *loved*. They each felt like the only person in the room.

That's God.

That's His style.

Jesus forgave people of their mistakes and healed their hearts, bodies, and minds, and He gave them hope and a vision for their lives. The truth He spoke—that each person is *seen* and *understood* and *loved* deeply by God—set people free. It changed them from being slaves to fear, shame, and inferiority to being children of a God who not only recognizes them, but also understands them and loves them just as they are—warts and all—and embraces them.

He spoke with the people no one would speak with.

~~~~~

He touched people no one would touch.

He ate and drank with people no "righteous" person would eat with.

He befriended and gave worth to the dirty and socially worthless.

You get the point.

He was God in human form, and it seemed that when He was around people, either their hearts would swell as they felt loved in His presence, or they would feel deeply threatened because His love for everyone didn't fit into their religious framework and understanding of who they thought He was.

Heather sometimes says that she feels sorry for God because He is so often misunderstood and misrepresented. I always smile when she says that because I don't think God needs our pity. But I do think she's right about Him being misunderstood.

God is all about *relationship*. That's what He's been trying to communicate and invite humanity into since the beginning. He wants us to relate to Him by allowing Him to show us that He sees us, understands us, loves us, and believes we are worth being in a relationship with. He wants this key relationship with Him to spill over into all our other relationships.

Do you get it? Sure you do.

Truthfully, it's really simple. Simple enough for children to understand.

Jesus said, "Come to me like a child."

He knew that as we get older, we would somehow get it in our heads that it can't be as simple as being like children who trust and enjoy their dad. Jesus knew that we can become cynical and hardened and get the idea that it's got to be more complicated than that.

Jesus knew that our earthly fathers wouldn't always do the best job displaying for us what God the Father is like. I get this because I know that as much as I want to be the perfect dad for my kids, I'm not. I'm definitely the man for the job, but I also know that I let them down sometimes, whereas God never lets us down.

Maybe your father scared or abused you.

Maybe he expected you to live up to impossibly high standards so you felt you were never good enough.

Maybe he abandoned you.

Whatever the case may be, there is only one perfect Father. Jesus came to earth to show humanity firsthand what God the Father is like.

One of Jesus' disciples, Philip (fine name), asked Jesus, "Show us the Father." And Jesus said, "If you have seen me, you have seen the Father" (John 14:8–9 CEV). Basically Jesus said to Philip: "Ta-da . . . surprise! If you're looking at me, you're looking at God!"

God is

LOVING

JOYFUL

PEACEFUL

PATIENT

GENTLE

GOOD

KIND

CALM

FORGIVING

COMPASSIONATE

and can't stand anything that separates us from Him because He knows that life with Him in the center is the very best thing for us.

If your understanding of who God is—and what He is like—is different from who Jesus is and what He displayed for us, then you have the wrong idea. And if you have the wrong idea about who God is, it'll cause you to keep a distance. You're gonna be afraid of Him, the way Heather was afraid of her dentist.

Hear me: I follow Jesus not because I'm scared of Him, but because He's amazing and He knows me—the *actual* me. He gets me and loves me. He sees, gets, and loves you too. That's what God is like.

Inside you is a simple childlike understanding that's telling you, you are valuable and loved by God, who is a really, really *good* God—a "just like Jesus" God—and you can trust Him.

I follow Jesus
not because I'm
scared of Him, but
because He's amazing.

8

WE'RE ALL MEANT TO BE

My birth mother was only seventeen years old when she had me, and she did an incredibly brave thing by allowing me to be adopted as a baby. I guess when I think about it, society would technically consider me to be a mistake. Growing up I wrestled with feeling like that was true, that maybe I wasn't meant to exist. But now I know better, and you need to hear me, hear me really good: I am no mistake and neither are you, no matter who you are or where you've come from.

~~~~~~

Whether you're an adopted kid like me or a foster kid or someone who feels unwanted or not valued, let me tell you the truth: you and me are the same—fearfully and wonderfully made. And God has wild plans and purposes for each of us. Our existence here on earth was planned out, anticipated, and celebrated by God long before we arrived down here.

You're no biological blunder or merely the result of a backseat fumble between two people looking for love in all the wrong places. You're not a mistake. No, you're meant to be here on this planet for such a time as this, just like I am, just like everyone else here. Maybe you don't feel it most of the time.

Maybe you've never been told who you truly are. If you haven't been told who you are, then you've probably filled in the gaps with wrong ideas about yourself.

Like:

I'm so stupid. How could I do that?
I'll never amount to anything.
Why do I even try?
People are gonna figure out that I'm a loser.

~~~~~

I'm dirty.
My life is worthless . . . blah, blah.

I could go on, but I don't need to because we all know these lines or lines like them. Let the One who made you tell you who you really are . . . golden . . . yup, a Golden Child.

This is who you actually are—this is the actual you, and you are inexplicably valuable.

You've been known and loved since before the world ever spun in the galaxy. You are loved and valuable and of such great worth that the One who made you calls you—and me—*beloved*! This isn't just some kind of power-of-positive-thinking technique to make us feel like our time on earth isn't a waste of time and we are actually significant. This is the truth! If it's not the truth, then I'm out. But thankfully it *is* the truth, and that's why I'm in.

I can hear some of you say, "You don't get it. He can't love me because I've done some seriously dark stuff. I'm sure He's angry with me." Well, yes, sometimes He gets angry. But if you feel at times like God is getting angry

~~~~~

with you, it's because He's actually getting angry *for* you. He sees the stupid ways you're going about this, and He sees you're getting ripped off because you're doing things that are hurting you and the people around you.

But don't worry, you're not alone in the "doing stupid things" category. We're all in it. We're all failures. But before that we're *beloved* failures. Everyone knows we fall for stupid lies that lead us to do and say and think the wrong things, but in spite of that we are still God's beloved.

Let me be the first to say that I've not got it all dialed in. I fail sometimes and dip into fear and anxiety and think, do, and say the wrong stuff at times. But my failures don't define me. And this is what I'm sure of: I was created a golden child who was known and loved before I was even born.

If we can just understand that we, along with every other living person on this planet, are meant to be here and are valuable and loved by God, then we might not see each other as losers or winners. But that has to start with you and me understanding and accepting this about ourselves.

But don't worry, you're not alone in the "doing stupid things" category.

I don't know what's been going on in your life, but God does, and He wants to walk through this life with you and me because He straight up thinks we're stinkin' fantastic! You might not know it yet, but He does. He knows it because He knows you better than you know yourself. He knows who you are because He made you and He really likes what He made!

Listen, I'm not a God salesman. He doesn't need me to give Him a five-star rating or two thumbs up, but I've gotta say, He's amazing and you can trust Him.

Do it! Do it! Do it! Do it—I double dog dare ya!

Okay, so here's what you might want to do. Put this book down now, put your phone on silent, and get alone somewhere so you can talk to Him. Go for a walk, take a drive, find a new location. Whatever you do, make it a place or situation that you can mark, and remember it as being the beginning of a new way of thinking and living.

There's one voice we truly need to hear but often can't because it gets drowned out by BLAH BLAH BLAH BLAH BLAH BLAH BLAH BLAH BLAH BLAH BLAH BLAH BLAH BLAH BLAH BLAH BLAH BLAH BLAH BLAH BLAH BLAH BLAH BLAH BLAH BLAH

~~~~~

BLAH BLAH BLAH BLAH BLAH BLAH BLAH BLAH
BLAH BLAH BLAH BLAH BLAH BLAH BLAH BLAH
BLAH BLAH BLAH BLAH BLAH BLAH BLAH BLAH
BLAH BLAH BLAH BLAH BLAH BLAH BLAH BLAH
BLAH BLAH BLAH BLAH BLAH BLAH BLAH BLAH
BLAH BLAH BLAH BLAH BLAH BLAH BLAH BLAH
BLAH BLAH BLAH BLAH BLAH BLAH BLAH BLAH
BLAH BLAH BLAH BLAH BLAH BLAH BLAH BLAH
BLAH BLAH BLAH BLAH BLAH BLAH BLAH BLAH
BLAH BLAH BLAH BLAH BLAH BLAH BLAH BLAH
BLAH BLAH BLAH BLAH BLAH BLAH BLAH BLAH
BLAH BLAH what? BLAH BLAH BLAH BLAH BLAH
BLAH BLAH BLAH BLAH BLAH BLAH BLAH BLAH
BLAH BLAH BLAH BLAH BLAH BLAH BLAH BLAH
BLAH BLAH BLAH God's voice BLAH BLAH BLAH
BLAH BLAH BLAH BLAH BLAH BLAH BLAH BLAH
BLAH BLAH BLAH BLAH BLAH BLAH BLAH BLAH
BLAH BLAH BLAH BLAH BLAH BLAH BLAH BLAH
BLAH BLAH BLAH BLAH BLAH BLAH BLAH BLAH
BLAH BLAH BLAH BLAH BLAH BLAH BLAH BLAH
BLAH BLAH BLAH BLAH BLAH BLAH BLAH BLAH
BLAH BLAH BLAH BLAH BLAH BLAH BLAH BLAH

BLAH BLAH BLAH BLAH BLAH BLAH BLAH BLAH
BLAH BLAH BLAH BLAH BLAH BLAH BLAH BLAH
BLAH BLAH BLAH BLAH BLAH BLAH BLAH BLAH
BLAH BLAH BLAH BLAH BLAH BLAH BLAH BLAH
BLAH BLAH BLAH BLAH BLAH BLAH BLAH BLAH
BLAH BLAH BLAH BLAH BLAH BLAH BLAH BLAH
BLAH BLAH BLAH BLAH BLAH BLAH BLAH BLAH
BLAH BLAH BLAH BLAH BLAH BLAH BLAH BLAH
BLAH BLAH BLAH BLAH BLAH BLAH BLAH do
you hear Me? BLAH BLAH BLAH BLAH BLAH BLAH
BLAH BLAH BLAH BLAH BLAH BLAH BLAH BLAH
BLAH BLAH BLAH BLAH BLAH BLAH BLAH BLAH
BLAH BLAH BLAH BLAH BLAH BLAH BLAH BLAH
BLAH BLAH BLAH BLAH BLAH BLAH BLAH BLAH
BLAH BLAH BLAH BLAH BLAH BLAH BLAH BLAH
BLAH BLAH BLAH BLAH BLAH BLAH do you want
to hear Me? BLAH BLAH BLAH BLAH BLAH BLAH
BLAH BLAH BLAH BLAH BLAH BLAH BLAH BLAH
BLAH BLAH BLAH BLAH BLAH BLAH BLAH BLAH
BLAH BLAH BLAH BLAH BLAH BLAH BLAH BLAH
BLAH BLAH BLAH BLAH BLAH BLAH BLAH BLAH
BLAH BLAH BLAH BLAH BLAH BLAH BLAH BLAH

~~~~~

BLAH BLAH BLAH BLAH BLAH BLAH BLAH BLAH BLAH BLAH BLAH BLAH BLAH BLAH BLAH plus more endless BLAH BLAH BLAH BLAH shut 'em up and listen.

Listen.

9

A LETTER TO ALEX

I knew Alex.

We weren't best friends or anything.

He was older and cooler.

We both wore glasses.

We went to youth group together.

Our youth leader gave us an assignment.

We drew names out of a box.

I drew Alex's name.

The assignment was to write that person a letter of encouragement that week.

~~~~~

I didn't do it.

On Thursday Alex killed himself.

I didn't know what to do with that.

I kept the whole thing to myself for a long time.

Alex, I really wish I'd written that letter, and I really wish you were still here.

I've been thinking about that a lot lately. I've often wondered what I would have written back then, compared to what I'd write now.

Alex's gone. He can't come back, and a letter from me won't bring him back. But I owe it to him, and it's about time I wrote it.

Alex,

I know we didn't know each other that well back then, and I wish we could have been better friends, but you were four years older than me, and in my mind you were way cooler than me.

It wasn't the usual shallow teenage stuff that made me think you were cool. It was because the few times we hung out and talked, you were always really kind to me, and it meant a lot. For

~~~~~

that, I looked up to you and always looked forward to seeing you at youth group or around town.

From what my dad told me after he spoke with your dad one day, you were pretty smart, and you were starting college and wanted to build things—big things like skyscrapers. I remember how that left an impression on me that you wanted to do something big with your life. At the time I had no idea what I wanted to do, and the fact you had a vision for your future made me start to think about my own.

I'm sure you didn't know it, but you left quite an impression on me, and for that I thank you. Without knowing it you actually cast a vision for me when no one else around me was doing that. You made me think beyond high school, which wasn't normal for me or anyone around me. I think we all felt like we were just existing and floating around, hoping to not be thought of as uncool.

So when my dad came into my room that night to tell me what had happened, it didn't compute with my brain, because in my mind you had your future all planned out, and you were going places. You were going to do amazing things with your life and become a "success."

I guess the truth was that you were wrestling with all kinds of things that led you to do what you did. After you died, I just kept my head down and didn't ask any questions about why you opted out of life.

The only reason I could think of at the time was that I didn't write the letter. As far as I was concerned it was my fault for not caring enough to put pen to paper and write something that might have kept you here.

I'm really sorry. I wish I could go back and write the most life-giving, encouraging letter to you, something that would have changed your mind, because you were really cool to me, and I looked up to you. I wish I could visit the buildings you would have designed and be able to proudly say, "I know the guy who created that building. He's a great guy and a good mate."

I wonder if you regret doing what you did. I

wonder if you could write me a letter today, what you would write? Somehow I think I know what you would say, or at least what I hope you would say. I wonder if it would go something like this:

Phil,

Don't beat yourself up over the letter. Honestly, if you'd written it, I don't know that I'd have even bothered to open it. And if I had read it, I'm not sure that any words you could have written to me back then would have changed what really needed to change inside of me, because what really needed to change wasn't the depression or shame or . . . fill in the blank.

I had my issues for sure, and they were very real and very dark, but they weren't the root issue. The root issue was deeper and bigger, and it affected every area of my life.

Of course I know it now, but I really wish I could have known it back then. The issue was this: my eyes didn't work. I couldn't see things properly. I remember back then how we both wore glasses, but I'm not talking about physical sight, I'm talking about the deeper way we see with the eyes of the heart.

The way I saw things at my core left me confused and disoriented and lost, which led me to a tragic moment that I regret because I threw away my life, and my life wasn't meant to end that way. It was supposed to have been lived so differently, but I didn't see things as they truly were. The truth was that I was a great kid, an amazing kid. But I couldn't love myself because I didn't see that I was always deeply and desperately loved by God. Even in my darkest, dirtiest times of despair and confusion and self-destruction, He always thought of me as His beautiful son that He was so proud of. Do you know why He thought that? Because He made me, and what He made was gold.

I see it now. I know it now. But I didn't know it back then. I let what I saw with my eyes and thought in my head shape my view of

~~~~~

my life. My view was that I didn't fit in and was worthless. I didn't see God as love. I saw Him as a disappointed, distant being who was disgusted by every thought I had and everything I did.

I was wrong. I was badly wrong.

I'm glad you thought I was a cool guy back then, but the reality was that I was terrified and hiding because I didn't want anyone to get to know me. I was afraid that if they did, they'd see me for who I falsely believed I was—a weak and disappointing person who probably shouldn't be here and who wouldn't be missed, and whose life would always be painful and hidden and would never measure up.

The fact that I never got to love anyone the way I was loved all along is sad. If I'd known what I know now, I'd have seen myself and God differently. I would've loved myself well and been able to love my friends and family and maybe even a spouse and kids the way God loves me.

Here's the thing: it's not too late for you. You can see things the way they truly are. You can see God and yourself and other people and the world through the correct lens. You don't need to be blind to the truth. You don't have to wait till heaven to have your vision corrected. You need to see God the way Jesus explained Him to be in the story of the prodigal son.

Jesus described God as a dad who was so in love with his kids that when one of his sons left home to go and get wild in the city, he didn't turn his back. Instead, he headed out onto the front porch, waiting and hoping for his kid to come to his senses and return home.

When finally his son did come to his senses after doing all kinds of stupid partying and blowing all his money, and hitting rock bottom—homeless, broke, and filthy—he decided to head back home, smelling like pig shtuff. The son hoped that maybe he could beg his father to hire him on as a farmhand. But when the son was still a long way off, he caught a glimpse of the family farm and saw a small, moving dust cloud with the silhouette of a man out front. It was his father, running toward him at full speed and yelling at the top of his lungs.

Surely his father was screaming for him to get off his property because he knew the dirty things he'd done and the places he'd been and the shame he'd brought on the family. He thought about turning and leaving. But before he could do it, he realized that his father wasn't screaming at him at all. He was laughing and crying at the same time and calling out his name.

When they reached each other, the father crashed into his son and threw his arms around him. They cried on each other's shoulders, and the father called out to the staff to bring fresh clothes and a gold ring to put on the filthy hand of his son, a kid who always had been loved so deeply but hadn't been able to see it until that very moment.

That's God. He's better than you ever thought He was. And that's why you wander sometimes—because you don't fully understand or trust that you're a beloved child of God and that you'll never be too dirty to be hugged and loved and told who you truly, actually are.

It's this kindness and beauty and grace and forgiveness that breaks us and turns us around. And just like the prodigal son, we won't begin to see our Father as He truly is until we make our feeble yet deliberate steps toward Him that we begin to see Him as He truly is.

This is the love Jesus described and offers— love you need to embrace and keep embracing while you're alive. Embrace it, and live and love yourself and God and the people around you as best you can with the same love you're loved with.

This is how it's meant to work: you give what you get, and that's why you've got to "get it" and guard it; guard it against lies that will bring blindness to your heart. Even well-meaning religious people can unintentionally misrepresent the nature of God and make you want to run and hide in the shadows as opposed to living in the light as He is in the light.

Phil, you are so loved and so valuable. You

and everyone you meet are seen, understood, and loved by God. Tell everyone.

Yours sincerely,
Alex

P.S. I don't need glasses anymore. How about you?

Note: I didn't start the letter thinking that it was going to be flipped and I was going to write a letter from Alex instead of writing one to him. It just happened, and as I wrote it I cried. I cried for Alex, I cried for myself. But mostly I cried during the retelling of the story of the prodigal son. It broke my heart again, and it healed my heart again.

Thanks, Alex.

Guard against lies that will bring blindness to your heart.

10

NEW DRUGS, OLD PROMISES

If you wish to see you must give up your drug. You must tear away from your being the roots of society that have penetrated to the marrow. You must drop out. Externally everything will go on as before, you will continue to be in the world, but no longer of it. And in your heart you will now be free.

—ANTHONY DE MELLO, *THE WAY TO LOVE*

Some drugs are easy to identify because they come in the form of pills, bottles, or other substances. But other drugs are a little subtler.

I don't want you to feel like I'm being a Debbie Downer, but there are a couple of really important issues I see in culture and in the world today that we all have to navigate and get dialed in if we wanna keep growing and flowing in the right direction.

Obviously, there are a lot of things we could point to, but I don't want to spend our time looking at all the negative things in the world. I would far rather talk about life-giving things, so we'll only focus on a couple of issues I feel are current and important.

The first one is social media. I sometimes call it social MEdia. (Get it?) And I guess it's time to spill the beans: I don't do social media. At all.

I'm imagining shock, disbelief, and confusion as you struggle to process this earth-shattering news. But it's true.

If you were to ask me to explain why I don't do it, I'd say, "Let's get coffee so we can have a good ol' chat about it." Or I could just hand you this book and have you read chapters 10 through 13. There are actually so many reasons why I don't do it, it's pretty hard to sum it up in a fifteen-second elevator pitch.

The reality is that for a lot of people social media usage has become a lot more than simple communication or entertainment. There's a chemical reaction in our brains that happens when we get the likes and positive responses to our posts, a tiny high that can become addictive. It's subtle. We're not usually conscious of it. But it's very real, and it's why we keep checking our feeds—to get little hits. The small high it gives makes us feel like maybe the next hit will be better, but it never is. It'll never be enough.

Again, what I'm describing isn't something we're generally aware of. But deep down we know that something weird is happening to us that makes it hard to quit. Right?

A lot of people immersed in social media become phantom versions of who they actually are, and they're being dragged off-course like the whale. Social media usage is at an all-time high and so is depression, social anxiety, eating disorders, mental illness, and suicide.

The small high
it gives makes us feel
like maybe the next
hit will be better,
but it never is.

Like I said, I don't want to be a Debbie Downer or an alarmist here, but could it be that this isn't a coincidence? That a lot people who are immersing themselves in and even trying to self-medicate through social media are also experiencing these conditions?

I know there's all sorts of debate about causation and correlation, and I don't claim to have all the answers. But I think it's worth investigating the link between social media and all these problems.

Before we do that, though, I want to be clear, I'm *not* saying that everyone using social media is struggling with one of the conditions I just mentioned. Of course not! Some people know how to use social media without letting it use them and that's totally cool. That might be you, and if it is, good on ya! But for conversation's sake, stick with me and don't skip to chapter 11 just yet.

Remember in chapter 5, when we talked about how we all want

to be **SEEN** / recognized

to be **UNDERSTOOD** / approved of

to be **LOVED** / deeply valued

Now, think about what the world tells us about what happens if we don't "fire up our socials" or keep them flashy and updated enough:

> If we don't keep up, we won't be SEEN.
> If no one sees us, no one will be able to get to KNOW us.
> If no one knows us, it will be impossible for us to be UNDERSTOOD.
> And if no one understands us or knows we exist, then we can't be LOVED.

Shoot. That sounds pretty bleak, like we'll lose everything we ever wanted if we don't keep on top of social media. And that's enough to leave anyone depressed, anxious, and disordered.

I've been told on many occasions by multiple well-meaning people that unless I start engaging with the social media platforms available to me, I won't be able to keep doing music. There will be no way for anyone to know about me or my band, Zealand, and no one will book us because they won't know where to find us.

Pretty much everyone from our booking agent to our record company has said that it's literally impossible to do what we're doing.

A week ago I got a call from my record company telling me (again) that unless Zealand fires up our social media platforms, they are going to quit working with us. My whole livelihood and what I've dreamed of doing since I was a kid sitting in front of my parents' record player is on the chopping block.

Not fun to think about. The struggle is real.

Right now I know you're probably thinking I'm a first-class idiot. But before you come to a final conclusion on that point, do me a favor and keep reading.

11

MY MISADVENTURES WITH SOCIAL MEDIA

So how did I personally arrive at this unconventional and apparently controversial decision to simply not do it?

A few years back I was invited to be a part of a big tour. I was really excited because I'd been doing my thing under the radar for a long time, and it was gonna be fun to play in front of a lot of people again. At the time I had a manager who told me it was time to fire up my socials and let people know I was alive and still making music.

This made sense to me, although up to this point I deliberately hadn't engaged in any form of social media because I was happy without it. I enjoyed my life and my anonymity. Anyway, I opened up an account and started making posts. In the first two days I got more than ten thousand followers. Okay, game on. Now I needed to keep them interested.

I got right into it and couldn't quit checking my phone. I labored to get my pictures and posts just right. I quickly felt myself becoming addicted to what people thought of me (*if* they were thinking about me) and how I could keep them from forgetting me. I was constantly trying to come up with clever things to say; creative, quirky photos; and deep posts and verses that would make people see how spiritual and wise I was. *Ewww.*

This went on for about six weeks, until my family sat me down to have an "intervention." They proceeded to tell me that since I'd been doing social media I'd changed, and they didn't like the new social MEdia me.

I was shocked!

I sat there stunned for about three seconds and then

responded with, "You're right, I don't like me either right now!"

I deleted the account. Ahhh, it felt good.

I stopped because I realized what a self-centered, narcissistic, anxious, and absent, nonpresent person I was rapidly becoming. I was out of the flow and was losing my actual self.

Kinda freaky how fast it happened.

If my family hadn't caught it and been brave enough to sit me down for a little butt-kicking, I would have just strolled down that merry road and morphed into an entirely different person.

If I'm always worried and thinking about what other people are saying and thinking about me, then somehow the light goes out in my soul. And if I'm always comparing myself to other people to see how I'm measuring up, then I feel myself slipping and I lose myself.

I felt my heart get sick, and it affected my mood and my sleep and my interactions with other people. I hated that feeling, and I won't become a slave to it ever again.

The suggestion from well-meaning people to fire up the accounts still comes up fairly regularly. When it does I keep coming back to the fact that I love being free and clear, and I've become more protective of my brain space and my heart space than ever before. I want to be creative and unencumbered by the opinions of the masses.

I love this next beautiful generation coming up, and I want to see them come alive and get a zeal for the actual lives they were born to live, not the virtual lives they're settling for. Sadly the reality is that this is the most depressed, addicted, medicated, and suicidal generation we've ever seen, and it's also the most socially networked and connected.

It seems the whole world is being shaped by the public opinion of social media followers. Even as an adult, when I was involved I felt the magnetism to change and do and say things I wouldn't normally do and say.

We've found ourselves caught in an enormous feedback loop—a classic case of "give the people what they want." Meaning that if you don't conform to public opinion, which has always been there in various forms but now seems to be inescapable, then you'll not be accepted, so you'd better do what they ask and give in to their demands.

Social MEdia comes at a high cost. We're trading in who we actually are for who other people think we're meant to be.

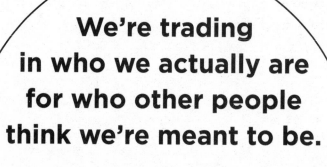

**We're trading
in who we actually are
for who other people
think we're meant to be.**

12

BEING A LOSER

» Consider This: the "Alternate Personality"

A kid posts something that is real and heartfelt. Only a few people comment or like it—his mom, third-grade teacher, and grandma . . . neat? The risk of posting something authentic that's met only with obligatory comments stings big time.

~~~~~~

No one *sees* him.
No one *likes* him.
No one *cares*.

The next day he decides to post something weird and random, a smart-alecky comment—not really his style, but who cares, right? No one's paying attention . . . or are they?

Three hundred likes!
Yes!
Seen.

That was cool. Hmmm . . . what next? He does it again. More likes. More smart-aleck comments. "Funny guy" just hit the airwaves. He's hilarious, crass, and kinda mean to people (only when they're lame and deserve it, though). Authentic guy can take a hike 'cause funny guy rules and people love him.

Dang.

I would have loved to have known that awesome kid before he morphed!

~~~~~

No one's paying attention . . . or are they?

» Consider This: You Are Utterly Magical (SELFie on steroids)

You've arrived. You are absolutely killing it. Everything you post is on fire. Any little thought you have, every little tidbit of wisdom that flows from your fingertips is as if it were laced with magic pixie dust. People love you because you are utterly lovable.

It's kinda weird how responsible you feel for the thousands of people you've never actually met who have been captured by your magnetism. It's like you're their hope, their hero, and their psychiatrist all wrapped into one. They're counting on you to be real, but not too real, cause really real is potentially fatal to your brand. If you're silent, will they be okay? If they're silent, will you be okay? No . . . no silence. Keep the pixie dust pumping, cause if it stops pumping, the emptiness will be deafening.

You are your full-time job. Everyone is depending on you to be you. It is a challenge to constantly have to think of fresh ways to be "real" so they can see how authentic and unique you are. Don't even think about

~~~~~

taking a day off because they might forget about your incredibleness and move on to someone slightly more incredible.

You face the daily pressure of coming up with unique, fresh, authentic content, tips, and advice. When all else fails, a super-cute selfie always works—people love that. The constant crafting of yourself is like a gremlin that always seems to be hungry for more, no matter how much it eats. And if you don't feed it, it will die. And if it dies, you'll be alone.

Rough.

» Consider This: the "Comparison Killer"

Got noticed by the cool people today. Felt good. Posting something ASAP so they don't forget me. Got liked. Got friended. Cool. Keep it up, buttercup. Wait . . . no new likes today.

Need to come up with some fresh material. I'll Google some ideas. Okay, just posted. . . . Oh, shoot . . . wait, that one has been done way too much. Unoriginal—it could be fatal to my branding. No likes . . . dang it.

They're on to me . . . I'm a faker. Everything is easy for them. I hate my stupid clothes. My car is lame. They're happier. Cool vacation—we didn't even take one.

I'm fat. Wait, that angle makes her look fatter than me . . . I think . . . can't really tell . . . why did she even post that?

I hate my hair.
I hate my nose.
Why doesn't anything work out for me?
I stink. I basically don't exist.
No one cares if I'm here or not . . . I'm invisible.

Here's the deal, comparison is a killer—a killer of who we are. Life is hard enough without immersing ourselves in a 24-7 competition with other people. It's tiring. We were never meant to be able to keep that up. We can't!

I'm getting really weary of hearing about beautiful lives being ended or at least dying slowly—people not becoming themselves—because they're busy comparing themselves to an unrealistic mob of virtual lives on social media.

God knows that envying someone else's life and wanting things that don't belong to us leads to discontentment, which causes us to miss out on our own real lives.

It would seem that God was onto something when He delivered the tenth commandment:

> You shall not covet your neighbor's house. You shall not covet your neighbor's wife . . . or anything that belongs to your neighbor. (Exodus 20:17)

Could that also mean, "Do not covet the hologram cyber lives of people you see on social media"? Because that's exactly what those apps push you to do: to compare your life with how you think others live and want to be someone you're not. How can you breathe deep and enjoy being yourself if you want to be someone else? *Not possible.*

But do any of us even have a choice anymore? And

as I've mentioned, a lot of people have told me I don't. And yet there's a feisty part of me that says, hang on . . . so you're telling me it's literally impossible to be a valid human if you don't use this stuff? Really? Okay, let's see if that claim holds any weight. I guess I've kinda taken on the challenge to experiment on myself to see if it's possible, cause how can I tell people it's possible if it's just a theory?

I don't want to be the guy presenting an option to people who need help to get healthy without first seeing if it is truly possible and then living it out. That would be like a doctor lecturing his patients about smoking—how it's really bad for them and directly linked to cancer and other diseases, and how in order to get healthy they need to quit—then ten minutes later, being spotted laughing and walking down the street puffing on Marlboro reds.

Yikes.

Confusing.

What a wild experiment it's been to not do social media! I'm not the cool kid on the block for sure, but I'm totally okay with it. And what is "cool" anyway? *Cool* can be defined in a lot of ways.

~~~~~

I think freedom is pretty cool.

I think being happy is cool.

I think becoming the person you are meant to be
   is cool.

I think uninhibited creativity is cool.

I think not being unnecessarily depressed is cool.

I think loving your life is cool.

And if that makes me a loser, then fine, I'm a loser.

But there are a lot worse things than having people think I'm a loser—like losing sight of who I actually am and losing my soul. And when I say "soul," in this context, I'm not talking about my eternal soul, I mean my soul here and now.

I mean losing sight of my real personality.

I mean losing my peace.

I mean losing my sleep.

I mean losing my contentment.

I mean losing my connection with God.

13

TAKE OUT THE TRASH?

So, in a rather large nutshell, here's what I'm saying about social media: It's 100 percent okay to switch it off and not use it at all. Let's at least put this option on the table.

Every one of us is responsible for our own lives and for what we let into our heads and hearts. We need to be smart and aware and brave enough to take extreme measures if we need to—and I think *a lot* of people need to.

~~~~~~

So if something is making you feel a certain way that makes you think and act like someone you're not, then TRASH IT BEFORE IT TRASHES YOU! Right? Heck, yes, I'm right!

And it's not just me saying this. A lot of really smart people are sensing the need to rethink some of the things we as a culture have immersed ourselves in.

Remember, we actually have a choice in all these things. You know that, right? You don't have to do any of it if you don't want to. No one is forcing you. No one's putting you in a wrestling choke hold and saying, "You must download this app and sign up and post . . . now . . . or else I'll choke you out!"

Maybe it's time to rage against the machine by closing certain accounts and deleting apps that have been threatening to delete our souls.

If there is something in your life slowly killing you and driving you up onto the beach and out of the flow, then go banana jam crazy and slam the doors shut and don't look back.

Do it . . . I dare ya . . . you won't . . . or maybe . . . ?

Maybe it's time to rage against the machine by closing certain accounts and deleting apps that have been threatening to delete our souls.

There's a scripture about this that is simply brilliant and brilliantly simple:

> Let us throw off everything that hinders and the sin that so easily entangles. And let us run with perseverance the race marked out for us, fixing our eyes on Jesus. (Hebrews 12:1–2)

14

THE OVERSEXUALIZATION OF THE POPULATION

I grew up in the eighties. We had movies like *ET*, *Back to the Future*, *Stand by Me*, the Star Wars trilogy, *Goonies*, and my personal faves, the Indiana Jones movies. BMX bikes were the coolest things ever. I rode a Redline, and my friends and I would go crazy riding everywhere and spending our paper route money on arcade video games and pinball machines.

We had cool digital watches with calculators on them, and the first home-gaming consoles were just coming out. If you were lucky, you knew a kid rich enough to have one, and you'd make friends with that kid so you could play cool new games like Donkey Kong, Kung Fu Master, or Pac-Man. We'd ride to our friends' houses, spend the whole day roaming around town, and ride home once it got dark or in time for dinner.

There was also another thing that was kinda common for kids in the eighties: dirty magazines. You'd find them on the side of the road after someone felt guilty and threw them out a car window.

Or you'd go to a friend's house and for some reason that friend would feel that you both needed to sneak into his big brother's room to see what he had hidden under his mattress.

This stuff didn't happen every day and the porn wasn't everywhere, but at times it felt like it.

So fast-forward to today . . . WHOOAAAHHH!!

Porn history lesson (you won't get this in high school, but you probably should): Back in the fifties a young fella who shall remain nameless and who is no longer alive began publishing a "slinky" little magazine and started the ball rolling. Well, in all fairness, the ball had already been rolling for thousands of years, but this guy made it somewhat more mainstream and somehow more acceptable.

The magazine featured lots of scandalous photographs, and it blew up and became a huge seller that started a revolution in sex-saturated media. But although porn became more accessible through the decades, obtaining it still took some effort. People had to creep around the edges of town to find it . . . But *now*?

Now it's everywhere. The internet has changed the world, and it's revolutionized the sex business by making porn as easy to find as making a few clicks.

It's looking for us instead of us looking for it, and it's the fastest-growing industry online. It's a multibillion-dollar business, and the people who manufacture it know just how to get their hooks into the souls of us human beings.

They know how the whole thing works, and they're counting on all of us falling for the fake-out so they can get us as young as possible and make as much money from us as possible.

It's become a big ugly beast of a machine, and it's now time to rage against it!

Here's what we know about the porn industry:

It is there to make *money*.

It's designed and scripted and acted—it's *fake*.

You're being *tricked*.

You're also being *rewired*.

Your *heart rate goes up* when you see the stuff, and the chemicals flow.

Your body creates a *pattern*.

Addiction sets in.

Shame takes hold.

Shadows form.

You *hide*.

Loneliness takes over as the hooks sink deeper.

Time is *wasted*.

The cycle *continues*.

It's the gift that keeps on *taking*.

This isn't just some zipped-up, prudish church-lady talk. The threat is real. We're watching humanity fall for the trick and lose itself.

The question these days isn't, has the porn machine affected you? The real question in our super-sexualized culture is, HOW has the porn machine affected you?

It's a machine because it's set up to work automatically, and it's all about making money. It's set up to hook the users (or more accurately the "used") and keep the subscription or advertising dollars rolling in. It's big business, and it's counting on the good old-fashioned chemical and physiological process of addiction to keep us watching because our eyes = $$.

Without eyes the business dies.

So the biological reactions necessary for healthy sexuality in the context of marriage are being twisted and used to trick and trigger responses that will create addiction. That's why so many people are hooked. Which brings us back to our whale: something caught his eye, and so he got off on his own and lost his way.

If this sounds like what's happened to you, if you

We're watching
humanity fall
for the trick and
lose itself.

keep trying to get away from this stuff but feel like there's a rope around your neck that keeps pulling you back . . . well, guess what, you're not alone and you're not hopeless.

You were born to be like a mighty redwood tree—healthy and drinking from the river of life, not the sewer of porn.

You were born to be free like a majestic gray whale that knows where it's going and enjoys the flow of its life.

You can and will experience the breaking of this addictive cycle and the cutting of that pesky rope as you cooperate with the Lord and His strategies to get you free. The fire of lies inside your head will get extinguished, and the cycle will end.

Listen to me: God's not angry at you if you've been looking at porn! He's angry *for* you because it's not real. It's a trick and you're getting ripped off and wasting your time and life, and it is creating a block between you and God and hindering your relationship with Him.

Remember the prodigal son in the story Jesus told to describe God? Remember how the father wasn't mad at his son but rather waited patiently for the kid to make a move toward home? And remember how the father ran toward his son and gave him the biggest hug, even though he smelled like a pigpen?

God wants you to know that you're His favorite no matter what. And the truth is, He wants His kindness to lead you to a rewiring and a renewal of your mind that'll break chains and bring lasting change!

In the next few chapters, we're gonna talk about real strategy to break the cycle.

If the porn machine has pushed you into the shadowy shallows and up onto the beach like that whale, then it's time to push back! It's time to break the back of this beast in your life.

To be right on the inside.
To know clean peace.
To walk with sure-footed steps on solid ground.
To feel fresh.
To be satisfied.

Achievable?
Heck, yeah!

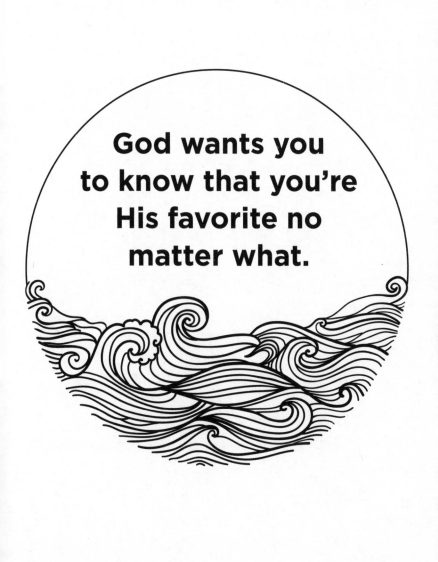

God wants you
to know that you're
His favorite no
matter what.

15

REWIRING AND RENEWAL

Be transformed by the renewing of your mind.
—ROMANS 12:2

Change your thoughts and you
will change your world.
—NORMAN VINCENT PEALE

I live in a 130-year-old house, and I love it. The only
drawback, until recently, were the old cloth-covered

~~~~~

electrical wires that lived inside the walls and ceilings. For years I knew they were a fire hazard and needed replacing, and I used to lie awake at night hoping no wires were getting hot and starting a fire inside a wall somewhere.

But I thought the only way to rewire this house was to tear everything out and redo it. It was going to cost a fortune and was going to be messy and would take months and months.

It wasn't until a few months back when we had someone come over to do some work around the house (I'm not very handy) that we learned the truth about how to rewire the house. The truth was that it would be a lot easier and a lot less costly to do than I'd thought.

The massive destruction and reconstruction that I'd been imagining didn't need to happen. Rather than tearing everything out and basically starting over again, all they needed to do was cut small holes here and there, cut off the old wires, and one by one, room by room, replace them with new ones. Ah, so much better and less messy than I'd thought. My house now has all new wiring, and I sleep a whole lot better.

〜〜〜〜〜

So how does rewiring my house parallel renewing our minds?

Well, first, it doesn't have to be an intimidating, tough process.

Second, it doesn't need to take a long time.

Third, it's about cutting off old lines that give power to old actions.

Fourth, it's about installing new wires or lines of thinking.

If we think something and respond to that thought the same way over and over again, it creates something like a wire in our brains. That thought will run down that wire and trigger an emotional response that then leads to a chemical reaction that then leads to an action.

So . . .

- Information presents itself.
- We respond with a thought.
- The thought is sent down a wire.
- The wire gives power to action.

~~~~~~

It's about
installing
new wires or lines
of thinking.

This is how "rewiring" works: When we start choosing to say no to the tempting thoughts and situations, it stops sending messages down the old wires, and our brains eventually cut off those wires because they're not getting used anymore. Our brains then create new wires to carry the right responses to our temptations. It's about consistently choosing to not send power down the old wires so our brains can create some new wires. Cool, huh?

We are created as habitual creatures, and we can use the power of habit to our advantage as we keep making the right choices. Our brains can be rewired and redirected and our minds renewed by the process of choice and repetition. If we allow the Lord to redirect our focus, then we can redirect the paths in our brains. This gets easier the more we practice it because eventually the old wires get disconnected.

Now, this doesn't mean we're never going to be susceptible to old temptations again once we've had victory over them and feel like new wires have formed. We always have to be aware that even though the old wires have been cut off, they're still in the walls, and if you really want to, you can connect them back up by making the wrong choices and allowing the wrong thoughts to linger. That will start the reconnection of the old wires and give them power.

So when a situation arises and we are tempted, we can choose to respond by letting our thinking go down an old wire or choose to stop it, redirect it, and create a new wire.

The process of reprogramming our brains is actually scientifically possible because of neuroplasticity, the capacity of the brain to develop and change throughout life, something Western science once thought impossible. It's just like the rewiring of my house, it's not as complicated and messy as you'd think.

It's one thought at a time.

That's why the Bible talks about "taking each thought captive to the obedience of Christ" (2 Corinthians 10:5 NASB).

This information is power.

Scientists tell us that it takes twenty-one days to break an old habit or thought pattern and twenty-one days to create new ones. It sounds like the science is now catching up with Paul, the guy who more than two thousand years ago wrote the letter below to people in Rome talking about the renewal of the mind. Nice one, Paul!

> Do not conform to the pattern of this world, but be transformed by the renewing of your mind. Then you will be able to test and approve what God's will is—his good, pleasing and perfect will. (Romans 12:2)

In other words, you'll be able to hear from God. Ah, yes, hearing from God—my favorite!

God's always speaking and communicating amazing things to us. He never goes quiet on us or gives us the silent treatment. BUT we clog the ears of our hearts when we're continuously in a cycle of sin, and that's why it's super important for us to practice taking control of our choices. God wants us to be clean-hearted and clear-headed so we can hear His voice.

Yes! *So good!*

I love being free to say, "No, I'm not doing things the way the world does things."

I'm gonna say *no* to the same old stupid
temptations that are trashing my soul.
I'm gonna say *no* to conformation and say *yes* to
transformation.
I'm gonna keep following God's brilliantly *simple*
ways of rewiring and renewal.
I'm gonna *keep* listening and *keep* learning and
choose and do and speak and love the way I'm
being loved by God.

We get good at what we practice. Habits form and new wires in our brains are installed that are helpful and healthy instead of dangerous.

Once again, let me say, "I stinkin' love this stuff. I love God's ways. They work!"

God wants to throw you a plan and a vision for your life and have you catch it and run with it!

He knows what's going on with you right now and

~~~~~~

knows your weaknesses and failures and fears. And He's not standing at a distance with His arms folded, shaking His head in disapproval.

He wants you to get excited about seeking Him and growing in ways you could have never dreamed.

He wants you to throw off the things that have been weighing you down and keeping you from running with strong steps.

He wants you to practice putting the squeeze on that old, burned-out wiring that has blocked the flow of His life-giving Spirit. And He wants to replace it with truth that will cause your heart to pump so strong and clear it'll want to burst out of your chest!

16

THE ESCAPE ARTIST

```
????        ????                    ????            ????
????        ????                    ????            ????
????        ????        ??????      ????            ????
????        ????        ???????????  ????           ????
????        ????        ??????????????  ????        ????
????        ????        ??????   ?????   ????  ????  ????
??????????????????????  ??????   ?????   ????  ?????  ????
??????????????????????  ???????  ??????  ???? ?????? ????
????        ????        ??????????????????  ???????????????
????        ????        ???????????   ??????????????
????        ????        ???????       ?????? ??????
????        ????                      ?????  ?????
????        ????                       ????   ????
```

When you are tempted he will
also provide a way out.
—1 CORINTHIANS 10:13

~~~~~~~

In the last chapter we got clear about repeatedly responding the right way to information and situations so our brains can be rewired and our old habits can die, right? Okay, the question then is, *How do we know how to respond in those moments?*

Here's the truth: If you've created a habit or addiction to pornography (or anything else for that matter), you need to know it can be broken. Actually, not just broken. It can and will be *destroyed* as you keep listening to the voice of God, who will *always* provide you with a way of escape. He will always speak and give you a way to choose to turn from the temptation and get away.

Every time you turn from temptation you'll grow stronger as you actively break the cycle by stopping the mental, physical, and chemical reactions in your body before they begin.

You get good at what you practice. If you practice resistance, you'll reroute the paths your thoughts have been following. And as you keep listening and doing what you hear the Spirit of God say to you, in those moments you'll experience the breaking of bad cycles

God will *always* provide you with a way of escape.

and patterns of addiction. As you keep tuning your ear to God's powerfully kind voice, you'll continue to become healthier and freer.

You have to start today and *take it one day at a time*. Learn this verse:

God is faithful; he will not let you be tempted beyond what you can bear. But when you are tempted, he will provide a way out so that you can endure. (1 Corinthians 10:13)

Question: What makes you vulnerable?

Is it times of boredom or loneliness or maybe when you are tired?

Whatever it is, the Lord wants to give you a simple strategy to cut off the attacks before they even start. Let's call this the front-end strategy. Chances are it will almost seem too easy, too basic, like "Don't have a computer with internet access in your room" or "Just go to sleep now" or "Get up and walk away."

Other counterattack strategies: "CLICK OUT" or

"SWITCH IT OFF." Yup. Most times it's gonna be that simple. The little X up at the top will provide an escape hatch, and when you click on it (as hard as it may seem to do in that moment) and escape, *it'll feel amazing*! That's a great feeling to get hooked on.

If a temptation comes and you ignore the initial escape route, and you feel triggers go off and fire chemicals in your brain and your pulse quicken, it's still not too late. You can still stop the attack even if you've let the process start. When the fight is on, you need to recognize and understand what's happened, so you can counterattack by following the *next* escape route that will *always* be provided for you.

It's in those moments that you can choose to either follow the escape plan or ignore the voice of God in your head and just roll with the cycle you've become familiar with. Even then, *there will always be places along the way where God provides turning points.*

Honestly, God's strategies are always BRILLIANTLY SIMPLE and SIMPLY BRILLIANT and are always available if we CHOOSE to see them and take them!

When the fight is on, you need to recognize and understand what's happened, so you can counterattack.

» It's Time to Shut the Windows That Let in Bad Voices, Sights, and Sounds

- It's time to *shut* the windows that have been letting in the junk that has caused your soul blindness and heart disease.
- It's time to *shut up* the voices that have been drowning out God's knock at the door.
- It's time to *shut off* the faucet of foul water that has falsely promised to quench your soul's thirst.

» It's Time to Work the Habits So That They Work for You, Not the Other Way Around

- It's time to *fire up* the habit of saying yes to God.
- It's time to *fire up* the habit of choosing life.
- It's time to be still and *listen* to God.
- It's time to *practice* remembering His presence. (Remember, we get good at what we practice.)

~~~~~

- It's time to fill ourselves with the *right thoughts*.
- It's time to fill ourselves with the *right words*, true words, His words: Jesus = the Word.
- It's time to let transformation happen.

Also, before you read on, I need to make something clear: *God isn't obsessed with changing our behavior.*

We all know that how we behave is important, but what He cares about most is the root issue: healing our hearts and getting our heads in the right place. As this starts to happen, our choices will become clearer and our behaviors will change.

» The Dude Gene

There is a prevailing idea in our culture that's been around as long as I can remember, but it's utter rubbish. It's the myth that somehow all males have the "dude gene." We believe that God slipped it in there, and it's the secret gene that every guy is born with.

It means that whenever anyone suggests we are

meant to live with purity and integrity, and that we all have the power to overcome sexual temptation, we all say "sure, right on, amen" followed by a "wink wink, nudge nudge" because we all know that it's actually impossible to resist because we're guys and we all have the dude gene, which means there's no way to override our genetic predetermination and turn from temptation.

If it's true that God put this sneaky dude gene in us, then He's mean. But here's the truth: He's not mean and there is no such thing, because He didn't create us as wild hormonal animals that secretly can't control ourselves. Why would He do that?

Sure, we're all hormonal beings living in a sexually charged world, but that doesn't make us slaves to our urges and impulses due to a secret gene. We can and must learn how to be in control of our behavior, but if we quietly believe it's impossible because we've bought into the dude gene lie, then it'll always give us some kind of license to be weak and give in, and we'll get ripped off at every turn.

Here's the truth: we are created with a free will.

It's what separates us from our pets. A hamster doesn't have the ability to choose right from wrong. We do. It's that simple. No secret gene can override this truth.

Kill that lie!

17

CHOOSING TO CHOOSE

I have set before you *life* and
death . . . Now choose life.
—DEUTERONOMY 30:19, EMPHASIS ADDED

I know we've already talked about it, but I want to
make sure you understand how important choice is,
and what a gift God has given us by giving us the power

to *choose*. It's called free will. And as we determine to align our will with God's, we'll start to make choices that will lead to a deeper and more sustainable healthy life, one lived with Him in the center.

So let's take a quick look at some of the areas we get to choose that will lead to greater life and freedom.

» You Get to Choose

If the people you're hanging with are rolling in wrong directions that take your head and heart to bad places, then you need to be courageous enough to get some distance from them. Sometimes it's people, and sometimes it's devices. *Being courageous isn't always about what you do. Often it's about what you don't do.*

» You Get to Choose

If you have a phone with internet access, which is now pretty much everyone, and if it's messing you up, then it might be time to disable the browser.

~~~~~

If you have a computer, tablet, or other device that follows you into your room and leads you down dark paths, you can choose to not let it in. Leave it outside. Now, I know these choices seem really basic and aren't the final solution, because the ultimate solution is getting our heads and hearts in the right place. But, it's where we start. It's kinda like if someone you knew had a drug problem and wanted to get healthy, you'd advise them to start by choosing to empty their pockets of drugs and clear the house as well, right?

Think of it this way: If you were the captain of a ship that was starting to sink, you'd first plug the holes where the water was coming in. Next, you'd figure out what had happened and make sure you didn't follow the same course back to the rocks or reef or whatever it was that you hit.

You'd then work on getting the ship repaired and strong again, and you'd be careful not to sail in those same waters again and set a new course. But first things first—you'd block the leaks first, right? That's what choosing to secure the devices that are letting in the foul water is about.

I know it sounds too simple, and I know it's not the heart issue, but it's the right place to start. *Make some practical moves to stop the patterns that start you on the wrong course.*

It'll take some courage, and maybe people will think you're weird. But *it's better to be weird and alive* than "normal"—breathing shallow on the beach with all the other people who are afraid to be weird and alive.

Not a fun party!

We get good at what we practice, so we're gonna practice making the right choices.

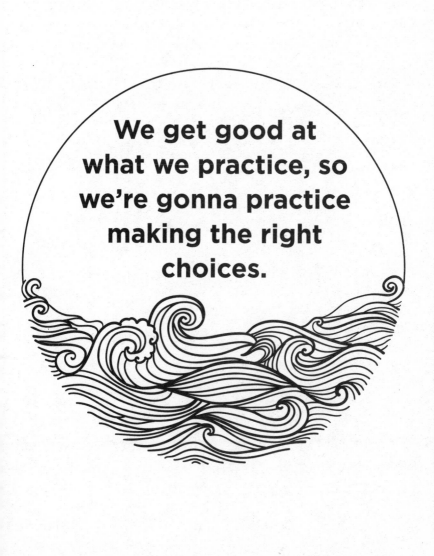

We get good at what we practice, so we're gonna practice making the right choices.

18

A HAIRCUT + A HERO = MY MULLET + JOSIAH

When I was a teenager, I had the best mullet haircut ever. I looked like a sixteen-year-old Joe Dirt. The voices of the eighties and nineties culture were preaching to me, and before I knew it, I was a disciple of MTV and FM radio. I followed as best as I could and trusted and obeyed their teachings on what clothes I should wear, what hairstyle I should have, how I should view girls and sex, and what I should want from them. They also taught me how I should view and treat uncool people—for example, people who didn't have mullets.

Anyway, I grew up a churched kid. I went to church on Sunday and youth group on Saturday. But somewhere along the way, the magnetism of the culture took a piece of my heart and left me with one foot trying to lead me toward God and the other foot trying to chase the things my TV, music, and friends were telling me to chase.

I didn't understand it at the time, but looking back, I can see that my heart got kidnapped by the culture I was living in and by the media I was saturated with.

My heart was split, and my allegiance went in two directions. I wish I'd been told there was another way, because at some point I needed to take responsibility for my life and decide to stand up against the things that were standing against me. I eventually did, one night at a youth event held in our town hall. It was there and then that I made a big move and decided that my life was best lived in the hands of God.

The deal is, we all need to make moves and *decide* who we are going to listen to and who we are going to be.

Which leads me to the story of Josiah. This guy is one of my all-time favorites.

Josiah grew up in 640 BC, a wild time in history, with an out-of-control father who was the king of Judah. Josiah's dad, Amon, allowed all kinds of debauchery and depravity into his kingdom and died a twisted man when his son was only eight years old. He left Josiah to fend for himself as child king over a messed-up kingdom.

Josiah decided at a young age that he wasn't going to live the same way his dad did. He would follow God as best as he knew how and turn away from the evil things his father had done and the culture he welcomed. He didn't know much about who God was, but his heart was open, and he kept moving forward, eager to discover more.

Josiah had a rough start in life, but he didn't let the past or his current circumstances *define* his future. This guy had courage—real courage to go against the things the people around him had embraced and probably tried to encourage Josiah to do too. Josiah said, "No, the destructive behavior stops now, and it stops with me!"

He had strong resolve at a young age to open his heart to God and to turn away from the things he knew weren't right. And the thing is, he didn't really have any examples of what a godly life should look like, but God saw his heart and knew what he needed. God wasn't going to leave him hanging.

The next chapter in Josiah's story is amazing. He knew there was a broken-down temple in the middle of the city that used to be the place where God was worshipped, and he decided to have it rebuilt. But before they could do that, the site needed to be cleaned; the rubble and junk needed to be removed. While they were doing this, someone found an ancient book and brought it to Josiah.

Josiah had someone read from the book, and the reading made him weep because what they had rediscovered after many years of neglect and after generations of wickedness was the Bible (at least the first part of it). Ignored and forgotten for many years, it was now being read to this young king, who couldn't believe what he was hearing and how it made him feel.

He was sixteen at the time.

God began to speak to Josiah through Scripture, and it changed his whole worldview. He decided to trash everything in his kingdom and in his life that was in opposition to God. He went for it and made sure *all* the trash was taken out!

Josiah chose on his own to follow God, listen to His voice, and get rid of the things that threatened to destroy him and that had, in fact, destroyed his parents and messed up everyone around him. He made a decision, the right decision, and he followed it by taking the right action—and things began to change in his life.

Here's the thing: you can be like this guy! The responsibility is yours and yours alone. You need to decide you are going to do things God's way, whether or not you have a spiritual example or role model. This is your life and your time in history, and whether you grow like a redwood or roam off course like the tragic whale is yours to choose.

Having other people around is helpful, and I believe God wants to lead you to people who will help strengthen you, but don't let your lack of spiritual mentors prevent you from pursuing God here and now. Start

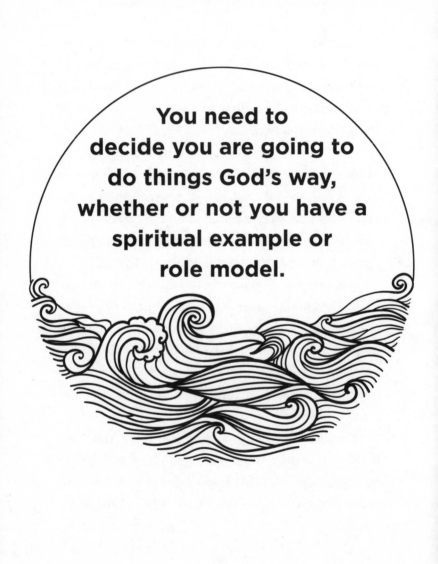

You need to
decide you are going to
do things God's way,
whether or not you have a
spiritual example or
role model.

chasing Him now and trust that He will provide what you need.

You get to choose because you aren't forced to be a victim of your circumstances—of the culture or of your hormones or of your family history or of anything else. You and only you can decide where your head and your heart are going to lead you.

You decide, remember?

Don't let the voices of culture that are loud on social media decide for you. Don't let the seductive sirens of porn tell you what's "normal" and what you should want and how you should see other people.

You decide.

I heard someone once say that a person's true character is defined by who he or she is when no one is looking.

As people who live in a culture that seems to be trying to rob us of our true character, we need to know that we can be the people God sees us as, people who walk out lives of integrity and who don't dwell in shadows and harbor secret sins. We can be strong like Josiah, who didn't allow the failures of history to define his

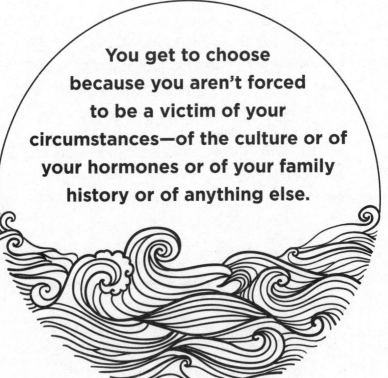

**You get to choose
because you aren't forced
to be a victim of your
circumstances—of the culture or of
your hormones or of your family
history or of anything else.**

future. And we will not allow the failures of our parents and friends or the culture and circumstances to tell us who we are or try to define us.

Josiah continued to follow God, and he *changed the culture* around him instead of the culture changing him.

Josiah, if I wore a hat, I'd take it off for you right now. I'd throw it in the air and yell something in a fancy British accent, like "Bravo!" or "Hoorah!" or something like that. Anyway, the point is, you stinkin' rule, and we're going to follow your example.

19

THE ADD
POSTER CHILD

Have you ever walked into a room and not remembered why you walked into the room? Me too! But the thing is, I didn't make it to the room because I forgot where the room was and . . . what are we talking about again?

Hey, ya wanna get coffee?

Do you like the asparagus?

Look—squirrel!

When Heather was pregnant with Phyn, she came

~~~~~

to me one day and said, "I need to ask you something. Will you go to a doctor with me and have him evaluate your ADD? We're having a baby, and I don't want you to miss this. I want you to be present, really present."

I agreed to go. But I didn't need a doctor to tell me I had attention issues, it was obvious. I'd struggled my whole life to stay on task and do anything for longer than seven seconds. And being in a successful rock band, where I didn't have any real responsibilities other than to play, sing, and jump around each night, didn't help either.

I figured if a doctor could help me be a little more present and not walk off halfway through unloading the dishwasher, then that would be a good thing.

So off we went. The doctor had me fill out a questionnaire and answer a few questions. After the testing and questioning, she said she'd never come across anyone who so perfectly fit the description of someone with adult ADD, and that someone should put me in the textbooks as the poster child.

It was weird. She actually seemed a little excited that she'd found such a perfect specimen. Her enthusiastic diagnosis gave me comfort. I felt understood. And the label "ADD poster child" completely validated my lifelong struggles.

The doctor prescribed medication and sent us on our way. I picked up the prescription, twisted the lid off the bottle, and popped my first pill. By the time I got home, it was working.

It worked so well that it actually made me tear up, because I couldn't believe this was how people functioned. I felt like I'd been missing out on so many experiences and conversations and opportunities because my mind was always drifting. Now, with the drug, I could focus.

I could focus on anything and everything and it was AMAZING. If I wanted to, I could stare at a crack in the sidewalk for an hour, closely examining it and finding it earth-shatteringly interesting. My songwriting was at a new all-time fevered pitch. Instead of working a little while and then getting distracted, I was now able to sit and write all day and all night.

Who even needed sleep? No sleep for me, thanks. I could sit and focus on a task for so long it was incredible. I thought that if this was normal humanity, I'd been missing out, and now I was catching up.

Needless to say, not long after I started taking my new wonder pill, Heather started to freak out a little. To be honest, I was acting really weird. I'd become so focused that it was annoying. When she asked me to go to the mall with her, I became so focused I could out-shop a Kardashian. A simple trip to the grocery store would take an hour because I'd become fascinated with the fine print on the labels.

If I took the medication too late in the day, I'd be up for hours wanting to talk and talk and talk, and the fact that I could outtalk Heather was a massive red flag of official weirdness. One problem had been fixed, but another, even more annoying problem, had emerged.

Dang.

A few months after my love affair with the pre-scription drug began, Heather and I had an encounter with God that sent us on a new trajectory in life. We had a life-changing experience with Him, a powerful encounter that prompted us to get up each morning and meet with Him before the day began. We went to different rooms in the house but did the same thing: we prayed and opened up our Bibles and asked the Lord to speak and become more real to us.

Guess what?

He did become more real to us, and we began to change. Old ideas and practices, thoughts and fears, began to fall away and get replaced by God's ideas and truth. He started rewiring our minds and transforming our thinking. Then something amazing happened.

At a certain point I decided to stop taking the medication. And I found that my mind kept operating as if I were still on the drug, except now I wasn't having to deal with the side effects of extreme highs and lows, annoying hyper-focus, or the paranoia and weirdness.

As I consistently practiced being in God's presence, talking to Him and allowing Him to talk to me, I began to think, see, and operate differently—all without drugs.

Miraculous, right?

This wasn't an overnight thing for me. It took me being consistent and practicing being in the presence of God.

God showed me that I had actually been a guy who could concentrate and stay present all along. That that's the actual me, but I didn't know it because at some point early on I'd gotten pegged as the flighty, spontaneous type. People had told me I was like that, and eventually I'd told it to myself. It became a part of my identity, and I thought it was hardwired and I could never change.

It was a label that I thought gave me the right to embrace my behavior and claim it as part of my DNA.

I know better now, of course, I just needed to spend enough time with God for Him to show me who I actually was and replace my old, faulty ways of thinking. It took a little time, but the change has been amazing. No wonder I'm hooked on spending the first part of my day focused on God and His presence.

Before I go on about this, I want to be clear that what I'm talking about here—spending time with the Lord—isn't a religious activity or just another Christian box to check to get on God's good side. This is just kinda logical stuff. It's about slowing down and building a relationship with the One who made us and loves us most.

As I look back over my life before I adopted this practice, I can see how my mind was never challenged to step into how it was designed to function with focus and direction.

I had never let myself slow down long enough and consistently enough for God to reset my focus and realign my mind to operate as it was designed to.

You might relate to not being able to focus, or you may have experienced something traumatic that preoccupied a large part of your mind and caused you to not think and function with clarity and focus. If so, I hope my story will point you toward God, who wants to show you who you are and how you were intended to use your mind.

He really can do this for you.

First, He wants you to bring Him your fears and your concerns and your true inner self, even if you don't know who you really are yet. He wants you to talk to Him about everything that's going on in you and around you—the good and the bad and the ugly.

Second, He wants you to be consistent in bringing all of who you are into the presence of who He is. And that means learning, as He tells us in Psalm 46:10, to "be still, and know that I am God." When we slow down and

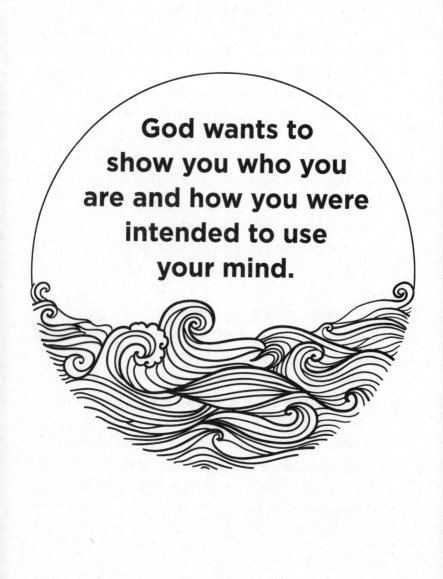

God wants to
show you who you
are and how you were
intended to use
your mind.

submit our thoughts to God through prayer and meditation on truth, then our minds can become renewed and aligned with who He is and who He created us to be—who we actually are and not who our thoughts and our surroundings and conditioning have misdirected us to become.

This is why prayer is so cool and so important in our daily lives. Even Jesus kept it at the top of His priority list. Praying kept Him in communication with His Father, who in return, kept Jesus in touch with who He actually was.

Obviously, as humans we are always changing and growing and becoming who we are. So this is not a one-time cure-all experience of praying a magic prayer. Rather, it's a lifetime adventure relating to our Creator and being led by aligning our hearts and minds with Him. This is what Paul meant when he wrote this in his second letter to the Corinthians:

We demolish arguments and every pretension that sets itself up against the knowledge of God,

~~~~~~~

and we take captive every thought to make it obedient to Christ. (2 Corinthians 10:5)

Drawing near to God and thinking as He directs the minds He created is how we demolish the lies and the pretentious thinking that have shaped our false ideas for too long.

We want to know God, and we want to know who we are, so we take control over our thought lives. And that begins with stillness and surrender and prayer.

It's so simple it's almost laughable.

20

WE ALL NEED THE ODD RESCUE

God is our harbor and our strength,
a very present help in trouble.
—PSALM 46:1 BBE

Surfing in New Zealand is amazing, but it's not as consistent as in other parts of the world like Australia or Hawaii. You have to chase the waves a little bit, which

~~~~~

means you need to know where the best waves might be and get yourself there ASAP. I had heard about an isolated surf spot at Murawai Beach that was only accessible by sandy forestry roads. One Saturday morning I decided I was going to check it out.

I threw my board in the back of my mustard-colored Austin Maxi, a very non-hip car back then that's probably supercool now, and headed off to this mystery surf spot. I went by myself, assuming there would be a few guys out there already. But when I arrived, I found that I was alone.

The waves were big and powerful and looked beautiful. I was excited but also kinda nervous about being alone and so far away from anything and anyone, especially in such big surf.

I'd driven so far on those wild forestry roads—in my two-wheel-drive car on roads made for 4x4s—that there was no way I was gonna turn around and go home. I pushed the many warning voices out of my head and jumped into my wet suit, strapped the leg rope around my ankle, and headed out.

The surf was big and powerful, and once I got past

the breakers and out to the big waves, I waited for the perfect set to come and eventually it did. I picked my wave and began to paddle.

I misjudged how this wave was gonna break and instead of catching it, it caught me. It picked me up and threw me down like a toy into a toy box and then held me under. Finally, the wave let me go and I popped up like a cork, gasping for air.

But before I could catch a breath, another huge wave broke right on top of me, and it held me underwater and spun me around like I was a sock in a washing machine. I remember feeling like I might black out, but I knew I couldn't because that would be really bad. I pushed through and fought my way to the surface again.

The way the currents were working held me in the drop zone for what felt like hours, and no matter how hard I swam I couldn't get away from wave after enormous wave breaking on top of me. Each wave would hold me down and give me a beating as if it were waging a personal vendetta. Again and again I had to hold my breath and fight to get back to the surface.

It was exhausting. At one point the waves relented

and I was given a long enough break to float on my back and breathe, but before I could even think about swimming for shore another set came crashing on top of me and the whole cycle repeated.

This kept going until I was so beat up and depleted that I remember feeling like this was it, this was the end. I had zero energy left and not an ounce of fight in me.

I began to think about all the things I was never going to get to do. I thought about my parents and wondered if they'd find my body or if I'd just be washed out into the Pacific Ocean. I had nothing left and could barely keep my head above the water. Finally, my feet began to drop and I started to sink.

This was the end.

I gave up.

I was so exhausted and annoyed that this was how my life was going to end that what happened next didn't compute with my brain.

I couldn't believe it!

My feet touched the bottom!

I was in water that was shallow enough to stand. I was saved. The tide had turned.

~~~~~~

I'd been struggling for so long that I'd lost my perspective and didn't know I was actually a lot closer to shore than I realized. As long as I could muster the energy to keep moving one foot in front of the other I was going to be okay.

That day taught me huge lessons. The biggest one being this: *help is always a lot closer than we think*.

There is nothing that God can't help you through. *Nothing*.

Maybe you're carrying heavy secrets.

Maybe you're hurting yourself.

Maybe you've been betrayed.

Maybe you're mad as hell.

Maybe you're lost.

Maybe you've been abused.

Maybe you're being abused.

Maybe you're abusing someone else.

Maybe you're pregnant.

Maybe you got someone pregnant.

Maybe you're addicted to porn.

Maybe you're addicted to a substance.

Help is always a lot closer than we think.

Maybe you're suicidal.

Maybe you're desperately lonely.

Maybe you're failing in school.

Maybe you're in a toxic relationship.

Maybe you're losing a relationship.

Maybe you're depressed.

Maybe you're hurting.

Maybe you're sick of rejection.

Sometimes we get into really, really bad situations and we find ourselves in way over our heads. The worry, the fear, and the struggle beat us up until we're so tired we can't see anything clearly, and we think that it's all over and there's no hope.

We hide and we wait for the next round of pain to fall, and we keep it to ourselves and don't let anyone get too close. In the exhaustion and the pain we lose our judgment and hurt the people we love until finally it gets too much for us and we surrender and give up.

There are only two ways this can go.

If we give up and sink into the hands of God in surrender, it's there that we find our rescue.

But if we give up and surrender to the shadows, we'll be consumed by loneliness, and like the whale, we'll breathe shallow and die slowly.

God is with you. He's right there with you, and He knows what you feel.

Reach out to Him. He'll reach back.

He will.

God is with you. He's right there with you, and He knows what you feel. Reach out to Him. He'll reach back.

21

SHUT UP AND TALK

In the morning, O LORD, you hear my
voice; in the morning I lay my requests
before you and wait in expectation.
—PSALM 5:3

I've been a musician for a long time and I feel like there must be an unwritten rule somewhere that says we're not allowed to wake up before lunchtime. I used to abide by that rule, but now I break it every day

~~~~~~

because each morning I need to be still so I can get my mind dialed in and my head on straight.

My process of meeting with God starts with getting up before the day gets noisy. I come downstairs to get a coffee and find a quiet spot to sit. My job has me traveling a lot, but I still follow the same practice when I'm on the road. Often there's a lot of noise around me, so I always carry earplugs to drown out the noise when I need to be still and focus on the Lord.

Personally I find that it helps to have a system to follow. For bunches of years Heather and I have been using a super-helpful reading plan, which means we can be reading the same things even if I'm on the road and she's at home. It literally keeps us on the same page.

When I start to read, I ask God to speak to me and show me things I need to see. When I feel something resonate, I write the verse or verses down and why I feel I need to pay attention to them. I then pray about what I've read, especially the things that click with my soul. I simply talk to God about things. It's not that complex. Just like any other healthy relationship, it takes time and communication.

Some people call it "centering" or having their "quiet time." Whatever you call it, it makes sense to do. This practice changed my life, and it needs to become a top priority in your life if you're wanting to get your head on straight. It's a daily recalibration where we get our minds in the game and focused on God, and it starts with being still.

Be still before the Lord and wait patiently for Him. (Psalm 37:7)

When we practice this, our communication with God starts to grow beyond a "prayer time." It becomes a lifestyle in which we begin to hear from God throughout the day. God's always talking and He loves it when we talk back.

Cease striving and know that I am God. (Psalm 46:10 NASB, emphasis added)

If any of you lacks wisdom, you should ask God, who gives generously to all without finding fault, and it will be given to you. (James 1:5)

So, moving forward, you need to know that we all have blind spots in our understanding of life and God and ourselves. That's normal. God wants to keep speaking to those blind spots and give us eyes to see Him as He really is, ourselves as we really are, and other people as they're meant to be seen.

And yes, there are things that need to be changed in our lives, but that's not why we come to Him. Don't feel like you've got to have your act all together before you can spend time alone with God. Remember, people loved being around Jesus because He could see them and know them and didn't make them feel judged and belittled. God is so good. When it comes to challenging issues in our lives, He's gracious and kind and patient with us, so we need to be gracious and kind and patient with ourselves too, okay?

We spend time with Him and want to get to know Him and hear from Him because He's good and His ways bring our real selves to life.

We are our truest selves with Him—our actual selves—and when we start getting used to that, our relationships with God grow and we begin to find ourselves operating in new ways. We find ourselves catching vision for our days.

This is about bringing everything to God and laying it out on the table for Him so He can share how He'd like us to think about life and the world around us.

I'm not talking about being religious and ignorant to our own issues or the challenges that are swirling around the world. It doesn't mean we're meant to jam our fingers in our ears, close our eyes, and go "lalalalalala I can't hear you!" as we try to shut out the real world. No way! Meeting with God does the exact opposite. It gives us clarity and aligns us with Him and His perspective.

Note: Something worth a quick mention is that it's really important for you to make these times deliberate and focused so the wonders of modern technology don't sabotage your efforts. It is so rude and hurtful when you're sitting with a friend, trying to have a serious conversation, and the whole time they are scrolling around on their phone, responding to messages, and so on.

Sure, technically they might still be listening, but they're not giving you their full attention, so you feel like they don't really care about or respect you.

It's the same with your relationship with God. Take it seriously and put your phone down or on silent during your time together.

Another Note: We need to be careful we don't find ourselves settling for a secondhand knowledge of God by trying to squeeze Him into our busy lives with inspiring music, podcasts, or YouTube sermons. Those things are amazing and can be incredibly helpful, but they're not meant to replace one-on-one time alone with God.

This whole idea and practice of meeting with God is kinda wild when you stop and think about it. The Creator of the universe and everything in it wants to take time to meet with us so we can encounter Him and get to know Him one-on-one.

It's crazy right?

I love it!

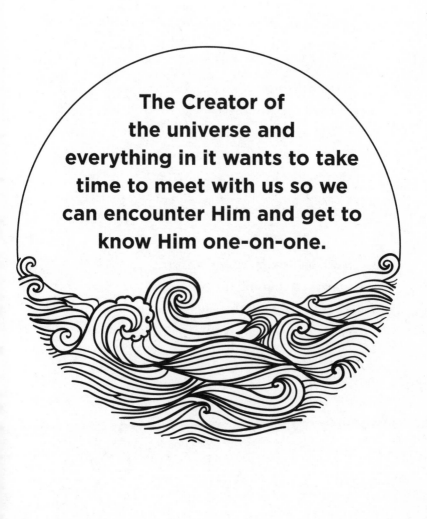

The Creator of
the universe and
everything in it wants to take
time to meet with us so we
can encounter Him and get to
know Him one-on-one.

22

BURNED BREAD = TOAST (STAY FOCUSED)

Technology can be our best friend, and technology can also be the biggest party pooper of our lives. It interrupts our own story, interrupts our ability to have a thought or a daydream, to imagine something wonderful.
—STEVEN SPIELBERG

Be alert! Be on guard!
—MARK 13:33

~~~~~

We NEED to keep our WITS about us. You've heard that before, right?

But what are wits anyway?

Why do I need them?

How many do I need . . . and where should I keep them?

If I lose them, can I get them back?

Can't I just borrow someone else's?

Ahhh, too many questions!

My brain meat hurts . . . can I borrow your wits?

Let's trade . . . I'll give you my five senses in exchange for some wits.

You work out the deal.

I'll agree to it.

And then we'll let everyone know about it via instaspam.

~~~~~

```
        IIIIIIIIIIIIIIIIIIIII
     IIIIIIIIII  SEE  IIIIIIIII
     IIIIIIIIIIII        IIIIIIIIII
   SMELL      you    TOUCH II
   IIIII                        IIII
   II  HEAR            TASTE    III
   II    _____        _____   II
    II      I            I    /
     I              )    /
       I      )_____  /
   _____ I          /_____
            ____ /
```

If everything is digital, then nothing is real.

If nothing is real, I don't need my senses.

If I don't need my senses, I lose my wits.

If I lose my wits, my soul slowly erodes.

If my soul slowly erodes, then I'm toast.

. . . and toast is just burned bread.

Okay, I went kinda bonkers there for a second, but what I'm trying to say is, *let's not get sucked in* by false voices and negative influences.

It takes work to stay focused and to protect yourself from being tricked or lied to or lured away from who you actually are and from your relationship with God.

Don't let the wrong things divert your attention. And last but not least, don't be a wuss! You need to develop a strong and vigilant focus that doesn't let you get easily distracted.

I used to ride dirt bikes, and one big thing I learned was that my eyes needed to be twenty yards ahead of where I was at a given moment. And another big thing was that where I focused my eyes was where the bike and I would go.

If I focused on a big rock that I didn't want to hit, I'd end up hitting it.

But if I focused on a section of the track that was away from the rock, that's where my bike would take me.

What I focused on would determine whether or not I'd crash into the rock or fly past it.

Sometimes I'd really have to fight hard to shift my focus to where it needed to be, but I had to because my skinny-guy bones were depending on my staying focused.

Don't let the wrong things divert your attention. And last but not least, don't be a wuss!

Let's keep moving forward and beware of time-wasting voices, either physical or digital, and of distractions that try to dumb us down and lure our focus away from the direction and flow God has us going in.

Let's keep our wits about us.

Finally, brothers and sisters, whatever is true, whatever is noble, whatever is right, whatever is pure, whatever is lovely, whatever is admirable—if anything is excellent or praiseworthy—think about such things. (Philippians 4:8)

23

GENERATION SMART

Rarely do we find men who willingly engage
in hard, solid thinking. There is an almost
universal quest for easy answers and half-
baked solutions. Nothing pains some
people more than having to think.
—MARTIN LUTHER KING JR.

Ｎone of us asked to be here on planet earth. But at
this time in history, with its unique issues and

~~~~~

challenges, we all want the world to be a better place, and we all want to be a part of whatever it takes to make it better.

I've heard it said that *real change starts with real people making real changes*. I believe that. But I also think there's a missing component in that saying. We also need to be brave enough to let God push our comfortable thinking around a little bit in order to see real change in our own lives first. If we truly believe that His thoughts and ways are higher than ours, then we need them in our lives.

I think we shortchange ourselves by not asking God to enter into our thinking about all things on all levels.

> Just as the heavens
>   are higher than the earth,
>   my thoughts and my ways
>   are higher than yours. (Isaiah 55:9 CEV)

Put everything in life on trial for its life. I'm not saying we all need to become urban hippies. But let's keep challenging what it means to live normal lives and

We shortchange ourselves by not asking God to enter into our thinking about all things on all levels.

keep pushing forward toward authenticity. And let's be brave enough to live in a way that brings us to the table and puts us in a position to be a part of God's solution here on earth. No one wants to be a part of what's wrong with the world, right?

And here's where things get really fun.

Each week when I'm out on the road, I meet so many amazing people who are taking hold of their lives, who are really thinking through some of the big questions, who are letting go of the things that are holding them back, and who are grabbing onto the real stuff.

I feel like the generation coming up right now is beginning to see through the fake face of the media-saturated, oversexualized, high-tech, and materialized world we live in and are beginning to respond to it by simply not engaging in the counterfeit.

They are wanting to relearn how to be human and grow from the ground up with God in the middle.

They are deciding to be like Josiah.

And they are deciding to be like redwoods, asking God how to live and breathe and teach them how to interact with Him and with one another, and this makes me really excited for them and for their futures.

Have a look at what God says in Deuteronomy. These verses aren't the intro to a self-improvement program about the power of positive thinking. No, they contain God's *promise* for you and for me—some of the same promises Josiah read and responded to!

> Now what I am saying to you today is not too difficult for you or beyond your reach. [It's not complicated or impossible.] . . .
>
> See, I set before you today life and prosperity, death and destruction. [It's your choice.] For I command you today to love the LORD your God, to walk in obedience to him, and to keep his commands, decrees and laws; then you will live and increase, and the LORD your God will bless you in the land you are entering to possess. . . . the land you are crossing the Jordan to enter and possess. . . .
>
> I have set before you life and death, blessings and curses. Now choose life, so that you

and your children may live and that you may love the LORD your God, listen to his voice, and hold fast to him. For the LORD is your life, and he will give you many years in the land. (Deuteronomy 30:11–20)

Do you know what that promise means? Your future awaits, and it's wild!

God has people He wants you to meet and work with and things for you to do that only you are equipped for because you were created to fit into the big picture whether you feel like it right now or not.

That's who you actually are: a perfect piece of the enormous jigsaw puzzle of humanity.

24

THOUGHT FOR FOOD

What if . . .

What if we kept asking God to show us more of who He is so we could really know and enjoy Him?

And He did?

What if we kept asking God what we need to get rid of and what we need to grab hold of . . .

And He did?

What if we kept asking God to teach us the sound of His voice . . .

And He did?

~~~~~

What if we kept asking God to show us where to be, what to do, and who to be with . . .

And He did?

What if we kept asking God to give us vision for our lives . . .

And He did?

What if we kept asking God to tell us how to not waste our time . . .

And He did?

What if we kept asking God to help us refocus our attention . . .

And He did?

What if we kept asking God to show us how to see and treat other people . . .

And He did?

What if we kept asking God to make clear His ways of escaping temptation . . .

And He did?

What if we kept asking God to give us new ideas and dreams . . .

And He did?

Because here's the deal: *He will!*

Oh man, I get so pumped just thinking about it!

Choose LIFE and don't let anything in your personal or family history keep you from choosing God and the life He has set before you.

Don't waste a minute on distractions and stupid things that will pull you away from the flow of God and His plans for you.

Focus on God and allow Him to bring you real peace, which will guard your heart and your mind.

No one's too young or too old to work this out and dial it in. Let's get our eyes set and our hearts planted in the right place so our roots can run deep and our thirst can be satisfied.

Let's keep growing and flowing like redwoods and whales! Preferably the non-beached, swimming ones.

Let's keep living in love with God, knowing that He *sees*, *understands*, and *loves* us.

Let's keep exercising our power to choose.

Let's keep God at the center of our lives and allow Him to shape our minds and our thinking as we keep enjoying Him.

Let's allow Him to run our roots deep in truth

Let's keep living
in love with God,
knowing that He *sees*,
understands,
and *loves* us.

as we enjoy our leaves getting greener as our hearts bear the fruit of a God-filled life . . . love, joy, peace, patience, gentleness, kindness, goodness, faithfulness, and self-control.

Yes . . . that's us: fruitcakes!

The world needs you as you actually are
you in God and God in you
Loved and able to love
"Love-able"
Thanks, and God bless!

ACKNOWLEDGMENTS

Okay, let me be really honest here, I have a real-life superhero in my corner. Her name is Heather and she's the greatest human being I've ever known and ever will know, and somehow I tricked her into marrying me.

Heather, I feel like having you at my side is like having an unfair advantage in life. You keep getting younger and greener and more beautiful and wiser and more loving and compassionate. It's your wild and unswerving pursuit of Jesus that's doing it, and it's just so dang attractive. You're not just my wife, you're my best mate and comrade in this experiment of life and faith and family. I look back and see that anything of worth in our life, or even in the pages of this book, we have hard fought and won together—you, me, and the Lord.

A strand of three cords is not easily broken.

You're my touchstone of sanity and reality in this totally unrealistic life, and I'm madly in love with you.

SNTSL (Sorry, secret code that only Heather and I can decipher.)

My greatest honor in life is to be your husband.

I want to thank my beautiful, creative, fun-loving daughter, Phynley, for being my strongest advocate in writing this book. You've cheered me on from the start and told me how excited you are to get this into the hands of your friends. Your encouragement always puts wind in my sails. Your creativity, passion, and talent keep blowing me away. Thank you for being my grimy drive partner and for having such a wild and adventurous spirit. I can't wait to see where the Lord leads you as you continue to grow and flow with Him.

To my son, Eden, who is zeal on wheels. Thank you for being so passionate about music and songwriting and production and for reinvigorating my love of discovering new bands and great songs. Also, having you onstage with me this past year was a surreal highlight of my life. The future awaits you, and I am so proud to walk into it with you.

I want to thank Joel Kneedler and Emanate Books for giving me the license to write like me. You trusted me and my style of scribbling and, in turn, you taught me to trust the process and gave me courage. Thanks for being brave enough to take on this project without me having a bizzillion social media followers. You caught the vision and put yourself on the line for a newbie author and for a generation who needs hope, and along the way I gained a new mate.

I want to thank the entire Thomas Nelson team, especially Janene MacIvor, your guiding hand and belief in the power of words is truly amazing. Thank you for working so tirelessly to make all the last minute deadlines and for believing in the words and stories the Lord has placed on my heart to put on these pages.

I also want to thank Brian Smith for believing that I was carrying something that needed to be delivered and for making that call to Joel. I think I borrowed your faith for a minute there, and through it my faith has grown. We serve a great God who can do whatever He wants to do, right?

I want to acknowledge Ben Eisner, not just for being my super pal but for giving me one of the key points in this book. We were talking about something spiritual one night (which is what we do a lot) and he said something like "every human being wants to be seen, known, and loved." That clicked with me and helped me see a lot of things more clearly. I've since asked him if he remembers saying that and where he'd heard it, but he swears he never made the statement. I'm not sure if he's just being modest or forgetful or just trying to protect my pride by letting me believe I came up with it myself.

Well, even if I did come up with it, I'm sure it came out of one of our many late-night chats, and I can at least thank you for all the inspiring Jesus-centric conversations we have had and for being such a stellar friend. Your life invigorates me.

Deb Hayes for being such a cheerleader and for your much needed critique and help with this project And also to Rebecca Conn for your comments, tweaks, and editorial snips.

Ashley Adcox, you have no idea how much influence you've had on these pages. God dropped you back into our lives at just the right time. Your affirmation of the content spurred me on and made it even more urgent. Thanks for spending so much time dialing this thing in and for helping me wrestle the words into submission. We love you and are so glad you're here. Oh, and thanks, too, for dog-sitting and for not corrupting the puppy too terribly.

I want to thank me ol' mate Mark Davenport. It blows my mind that after all these years and after all our world travels, we've ended up living on the other side of the planet in the same neighborhood. You've always had massive vision and have pushed me to see far beyond the impossible and to dream bigger. It goes all the way back to you pushing us both to start our first band together back in New Zealand, and your vision casting continues to inspire and excite me to this day.

I want to thank both my Zealand band mates and my Newsboys United band mates and crew for enduring me being a little bit aloof at times as I hid in dressing rooms around the country with my head down writing this book. Thanks for understanding that I wasn't trying to be antisocial, even when it meant that in order to meet the manuscript deadline I couldn't come four-wheel driving with you all in Moab.

I love you guys. We've all seen each other at our best and at our worst and it's made each of us understand and be even more grateful for the beautiful, indescribable grace of God. You guys are my brothers-in-arms and it's been a huge honor to travel so many roads with you over the years. It's been a wild adventure, and it just keeps going.

I'd like to thank my parents who have always cheered me on from across the seas. When I was growing up, you never reflected an angry, moody God who was ready to punish me, but rather introduced me to the depth of Jesus' compassion, which still today helps me understand the Father heart of God.

I'd also like to thank my American parents, Bill and Suz, who from the beginning were able to see past outward appearances and simply see a boy who was and still is crazy about their daughter. You embraced me from the very beginning with such a beautiful, open-armed, Jesus-type of love. I hope I can reproduce it one day when some punk kid asks me permission for my daughter's hand in marriage. I can only hope. The way you love God and people inspires me.

Most of all, Jesus. Honestly, to thank You in words is impossible.

You have taught me and are teaching me how to live and how to love.

You quench my thirst, and You leave me thirsty for more.

You are the river, and I love You.

ABOUT THE AUTHOR

Originally from New Zealand, Phil Joel is a Grammy-nominated musician best known for his position as bass player for the internationally known band Newsboys. His music has taken him all over the globe. Along with the opportunities to perform musically, he is a sought-after speaker, sharing predominantly with youth. He currently tours with Newsboys United and Zealand, his most current musical venture. He lives in Franklin, Tennessee, with his wife, Heather, and two kids.

For booking information contact:
booking@zealand.band
www.zealand.band